# RACIALLY MOTIVATED CRIME

## RESPONSES IN THREE EUROPEAN CITIES: FRANKFURT, LYONS

the **information** store

📞01603 773114
email: tis@ccn.ac.uk

## 21 DAY LOAN ITEM

*The Commission for Racial Equality*

*is working for a just society*

*which gives everyone an equal chance*

*to learn work and live*

*free from discrimination and prejudice*

*and from the fear*

*of racial harassment*

*and violence.*

Published 1997

ISBN 1 85442 201 4


Printed by Belmont Press

# CONTENTS

**Chapter Four: Rome, by Jolanda Chirico**

**Chapter Five: A European Perspective, by Ann Dummett**

# FOREWORD

In welcoming the appearance of this study, which I hope will prove to be of real practical use as well as interest to everyone concerned with tackling racially motivated crime, I wish to thank all those who have played a part in its creation.

First, the Oxford University Centre for Criminological Research deserves gratitude for its major role, from the earliest stages to the last: advising, encouraging and criticising. Its director, Professor Roger Hood, has given much of his time to the project, and his staff have been generous with assistance.

Secondly, the project would have been impossible without the support of outside funding, which has been received from the European Commission, the Churches' Commission for Racial Justice and the Lord Ashdown Charitable Settlement.

Advice and information have been given by many individuals, some of whom wish to remain anonymous: our thanks to them all, including those who gave very generously of their time in interviews with the authors..

Finally, the authors deserve appreciation for tackling an exceedingly difficult task. It is one thing to do a survey based on statistics and written reports, quite another to seek information through interviews on a matter where some of the people approached are unwilling to respond or have an interest in presenting a one-sided picture. The resulting study has produced many questions that need consideration by legally-constituted authorities in the countries of the European Community. With enlargement of the Community on the horizon, we hope these questions will be considered in the new member states as well as the old.

Racially motivated crime is one of the most serious and urgent issues facing countries across Europe, including our own. In Britain, we have learned from a great variety of initiatives over many years how difficult a problem it is to tackle. Unfortunately, its importance is not often fully recognised except by those directly concerned with racial incidents. I hope this readable study, which throws new light on international comparisons, will alert its audience to the dangers of an inadequate response and to the possibilities of effective action.

**Sir Herman Ouseley**
*Chairman, Commission for Racial Equality*

# PREFACE

As everyone knows who has had to tackle the problem of racially motivated crime in practice and come face to face with victims and witnesses, police officers and other officials to attend courts and visit the homes of victims' families, there is often little illumination to be gained from schematic surveys of the problem which begin from the top down. Looking from the ground up, one sees the difference between the way processes are supposed to work and what actually happens. The following study does not pretend to be a work of major, systematic research on racially motivated crime in general. Rather, it is a small collection of reports about what happens on the ground in a few European cities. Some conclusions may be drawn, but these accounts do not allow easy generalisation. The researchers in Rome and Lyons were often unable to obtain the data they wanted from official bodies. The accounts of interviews reflect the subjective judgement of their interviewees rather than a controlled investigation of entire divisions or departments of statutory services. The court cases the researchers describe may or may not be typical. Nonetheless, these accounts have great value just because they deal with the particular rather than the general. Only in the light of such investigations can we perceive where statutory frameworks may be faulty, the implementation of laws inadequate, and the intrusion of other factors into this form of crime crucially important.

The research was carried out in late 1995 and early 1996, and so it must be borne in mind that some factors in the situations they describe may have changed since then.

1997 is an apt moment for publication of these studies. It is not only the European Year against Racism, Xenophobia and Anti-Semitism but also the year in which the heads of government in the European Union have agreed at their June meeting in Amsterdam to give the Community powers to combat racism and xenophobia through police and judicial cooperation. 1997 could be a turning point in the struggle against racially motivated crime in Europe.

**Ann Dummett**
*June 1997*

---

The case studies in this publication are the work of the individual researchers named in the Contents. The views expressed in the following pages are not necessarily those of the Commission for Racial Equality or the Oxford University Centre for Criminological Research.

# BACKGROUND AND CONTEXT

Ann Dummett

## THE PURPOSE OF THE STUDY

The original purpose of this study was to identify good practice among the methods used in certain European cities to tackle racially motivated crime. Once such good practice had been identified, it could be recommended, in suitably adapted form, to cities generally; in particular, to their police forces, prosecuting authorities, public housing and education authorities, courts of law, probation services and voluntary associations.

In proposing the original plan, the Commission for Racial Equality (CRE) was aware that difficulties would arise in comparing different situations and the differing legal systems which had to deal with them. Racial violence in Europe as a whole is so obvious and serious a problem, but one so difficult to discuss at international level because of widely varying definitions and approaches, that an attempt at detailed studies in specific locations appeared well worth while in order to identify and learn from their differences. It was hoped that certain common patterns would emerge, enabling the reader to draw valuable conclusions, however different the backgrounds, to racially motivated crime in the cities concerned.

The original plan of the study, devised in 1994, was to commission in-depth investigations by different researchers in four European cities: London, Frankfurt, Lyons and Rome. The researchers would seek the cooperation of the relevant statutory agencies, interview officials, consult statistical records, study the literature available on legislation and procedures for dealing with racially motivated crime, consult national and local ethnic minority organisations to establish the nature and extent of such crime in the city, and cite case studies, in order to show, by example, how the system was working in practice. The effectiveness of the various authorities was to be evaluated.

Unfortunately, the coordinator of the project, who was to have carried out the London study and edited the book, fell seriously ill at an early stage of the work. The other researchers carried on, but the only material from Britain directly comparable with theirs was an unfinished pilot study carried out in Oxfordshire.

Even without this misfortune it would have been impossible to produce a set of four studies directly comparable with each other in structure and content. The difficulty of direct comparison is a matter of the greatest importance to any attempt which may be made in the future at international cooperation on responses to racially motivated crime. The problem is not that situations are so different that no lessons may be learned in one from another. The crimes and cruelties concerned are much the same everywhere. An innocent person is physically attacked, or terrorised with threats and insults, simply because he or she is regarded as a member of a hated group – racial, ethnic, religious or foreign.

In the following pages, 'racial violence' means all such violence and could include, for example: the beating-up of Muslims, the stabbing of a black schoolgirl, arson attacks on refugee hostels, deliberately running over a Gypsy, shooting at a group of Bangladeshis in the street, bludgeoning Jews, knifing an Italian, punching and kicking someone wrongly believed to be a Pole. The difficulty is, rather, that in each place the response is shaped and *perceived* against a background of specifically national and local history, politics, personalities, particular events, legal frameworks and customary habits of thought. Participants in these situations and responses take such familiar factors so much for granted as essential features of their problem that they simply cannot assess questions about combating racial violence outside their own particular context. A question posed by someone with a different set of local factors in mind may seem not to make sense, or may receive an answer not easily comprehensible by the questioner. And yet, fundamentally, the problems in two different places may be the same. A comparison, to be useful, must understand and distinguish the local elements in the different situations before considering what solutions can be generally recommended, or how general advice needs to be modified.

There are differences not only between the types of victim and the frameworks of perception in different places but between the legal means available to the various victims to obtain redress. It is much easier to compare the legal provisions in various places than to compare other factors. But the way in which legal provisions are actually implemented (or, sometimes, not) is another matter. To understand their application we have also to look at the kind of help available to victims, at victims' willingness to seek help or give evidence, at the measures taken for preventing violence in the first place, at the organisations and personalities involved in the whole story, and at the political background.

The studies carried out in Frankfurt, Lyons and Rome illustrate all these points. Yet another variation will be apparent to the reader; a difference of approach between the individual researchers. Their studies follow broadly the same plan but do not conform to a rigidly uniform pattern. This fact should be seen as a strength rather than a weakness. Any fruitful comparison of the responses to racial violence in different places is going to have to take account of complexity, before it can reach useful conclusions on general principles. Crude statistical comparisons can be misleading.

The pilot study based in Oxford provided the opportunity to formulate questions on the British situation generally. These, together with some information on the British background, are given below, to enable some comparison to be made with the completed reports. The pilot study's approach is based on experience of the British scene and on the assumptions current in

Britain about racially motivated crime. The word 'racial' is itself a stumbling block in international comparisons, just as definitions of crimes can vary between countries. In Britain, it is applied in the sense given to the term 'racial grounds' in the British Race Relations Act 1976, namely, grounds of 'colour, race, nationality (including citizenship) or ethnic or national origins'.

This broad definition applies perfectly well to the reports given below on Lyons, Frankfurt and Rome. But the word 'racial' often causes problems of interpretation when directly translated into other languages. And within Britain, in ordinary usage, it is usually taken to refer only to a difference between people who are white and people who are not. Racially motivated crime in Britain is occasionally directed against white foreigners, but the instances are rare. Overwhelmingly, such crime has as its targets people who are not white, regardless of their nationality or citizenship. (The majority of people in Britain who belong to non-white minorities are full British citizens.) Racially motivated crime is also directed against Jews and Gypsies in Britain.

Generally, racial prejudice and discrimination in Britain have the same targets as racially motivated crime. Racism is bound up with Britain's imperial past and with the history of debate on immigration controls. To pacify opponents of immigration controls, which, since 1962, have been deliberately aimed at non-white people, British governments have approved a series of measures intended to improve 'race relations': the three Race Relations Acts of 1965, 1968 and 1976; legislation requiring local government authorities to play a part in integration and the promotion of equality; and numerous reports and recommendations.[1]

It was against this background that a model for the present study was devised. Colette Smith's foreword to her report on Lyons clearly brings out some of the problems. She says explicitly, 'The greatest difficulty was to try to work to guidelines established for a British context which made little or no sense in a French context.' Jolanda Chirico does not make a similar assertion, but her report implicitly demonstrates not just the difficulty of using a British model but the difficulty of comparing the situation she describes in Rome with Colette Smith's account of Lyons. The German researcher, Anjana Das, had the least difficulty, because the British model of enquiry fitted the Frankfurt context quite well.

In fact, all the researchers have taken for granted, quite understandably, some knowledge of the national backgrounds they are dealing with. To assist those readers who may not be familiar with all the allusions and assumptions made, a brief commentary on each country is given below. First, however, comes a section on racially motivated crime in Britain.

---

1. For example, see *Racially Motivated Crime: A British Crime Survey Analysis*, Home Office Research and Planning Unit, Paper 82, London 1994. Local authorities have produced their own guidance, for example *Revised Racial Harassment Procedures (Public and Private Sectors)*, by Barry Simons, Director of Housing, Newham Council, 1991. The Commission for Racial Equality (CRE) has produced several publications including *Tackling Racial Harassment: A caseworker's handbook*, by Marc Jaffrey and Jonathan Stanley, London 1995.

## THE BRITISH BACKGROUND AND
## SOME CURRENT CONCERNS

As Robin Oakley pointed out in a report for the Council of Europe in 1991, Britain has a long history of violence against immigrants and minorities.[2] (He might have added that there is a long history of violence generally in Britain, contrary to the popular myth that we are a slow, gentle and law-abiding people.) But it should also be said that there has been a strong, countervailing movement of solidarity with immigrants and minorities among many parts of the population, even in periods of rioting against the unpopular group of the moment. The battle of Cable Street in 1936 was a confrontation between Sir Oswald Mosley's anti-semitic fascists and thousands of East End Londoners determined not to let them pass.

In the eighteenth century, London's poor often helped to hide runaway black slaves, making common cause with them against authority. Every measure of immigration control in the twentieth century has been fiercely, though unsuccessfully, opposed. The fact remains, however, that racial violence has often disfigured the British record. Since 1945 there have been a few highly-publicised incidents, like the Notting Hill riots of 1958, when black people were hunted down in the streets, but more alarming than these has been a succession of racial attacks, including arson, murder and serious injury, which have had little attention in the national press, though they get reported locally and in minority newspapers.

Official figures for racially motivated crime in Britain appear at first sight extremely high. In 1989, the police reported an average of six 'racial incidents' a day in London alone in 1987, more than two a day in the West Midlands and more than one a day in Strathclyde. Moreover, it has been estimated by the Policy Studies Institute that the several thousand incidents listed each year under-report the true facts by a factor of ten. However, there is a problem of classification here. Police records include *all* racial incidents reported, whether or not they are criminal offences. The incidents range over many kinds of behaviour, with racial murders at one extreme, and include arson, damage to property, personal abuse, threats, physical attacks, insults and graffiti. The Home Office takes relatively minor acts of racial harassment very seriously; the shouting of abuse, dumping of rubbish or daubing of graffiti on a person's property can arouse great fear, particularly because the victim will regard such acts as an expression of racial hatred.

There is no separate offence in UK law of racially motivated crime. Some immigrant organisations and others have been calling for some years for such an offence to be introduced, but opinion is divided, among those opposed to racism, as to the effects of such legislation.

Incitement to racial hatred was first made a criminal offence under the Race Relations Act 1965, which amended the Public Order Act of 1936. Complaints of incitement were to be made to the Metropolitan Police, who

---

2. *Racial Violence and Harassment in Europe*, Consultant's Report for the Council of Europe Community Relations Project, London, June 1991.

could then prosecute only with the consent of the Attorney General, who is both a Law Officer of the Crown and a member of the government of the day. It was rare for prosecutions to be brought, except that a number of black people were prosecuted (for inciting hatred of white people) in the first year after the Act became law. Provisions on incitement were repeated, with some amendment, in the Race Relations Act 1976, Section 70. That section was repealed in 1986, and the provisions transferred to the Public Order Act 1986. This makes it an offence to use threatening, insulting or abusive words or behaviour with the intention of stirring up racial hatred, as well as when in all the circumstances racial hatred is likely to be stirred up. The law also covers the publication and broadcasting of socially inflammatory material through media such as films, videos and sound records. Offences can be reported at any police station.

The Commission for Racial Equality (CRE), the statutory body set up in 1976, has the duty to enforce provisions of the Race Relations Act concerning unfair discrimination, but no responsibility or power to deal with racially motivated crime. However, its duties also include the promotion of equality of opportunity and good relations between racial groups generally, and it has therefore been concerned to provide information on racially motivated crime and to propose constructive ways of preventing and dealing with it.

The CRE is funded by, and responsible to, the Home Office, which is also responsible for the police and prison services, immigration policy and the promotion of good community relations. The Home Office has encouraged cooperation between voluntary and statutory agencies 'to play their part in creating a climate that is not conducive to racial harassment'.[3]

Detailed recommendations were made in 1989 to statutory agencies, including the police, local education authorities and schools, public housing authorities, the courts, the prosecution service, the youth service and social workers.

A 'multi-agency' approach was recommended, on the grounds that, for example, a family that was racially harassed by neighbours on a local authority (public) housing estate might suffer in physical and mental health, experience stress causing children to miss school or under-perform there, want to move house or need police help. Many agencies could then be needed to assist the family, and it would be useful to have cooperation on the case between the medical services, the school authorities, the housing authority, the police, etc.[4]

In Britain, some local authorities have introduced policies for dealing with racial harassment on their estates whereby the perpetrators are moved elsewhere. Others have moved the victims. In schools, it is now usual for a

---

3. *The Response to Racial Attacks and Harassment: Guidance for the statutory agencies*, Report of the Inter-Departmental Racial Attacks Group, Home Office, London, 1989.

4. The Government's inter-departmental group has continued to compile reports, providing detailed descriptions of how the problem is being tackled and what difficulties have to be overcome in different parts of the country. See, most recently, *Taking Steps: Multi-agency responses to racial attacks and harassment*, Home Office, London 1996.

local education authority to issue a policy on anti-racism, and some individual schools have gone beyond such recommendations to produce their own codes. In other words, there has been much voluntary cooperation within and between statutory agencies. However, the situation is rather patchy.

Why, when much goodwill, thought and effort are evident in Britain in combating racially motivated crime, are the British figures so high? One reason, pointed out in the pilot study on Oxford, is that the definition adopted in 1985 by the Association of Chief Police Officers in England and Wales (ACPO) includes not only racially motivated crimes but also behaviour which contravenes civil law, and actions which, despite being anti-social, are not unlawful at all. The definition of a racial incident is:

a.  any incident in which it appears to the reporting or investigating officer that the complaint involves an element of racial motivation, or

b.  any incident which involves an allegation of racial motivation.

Obviously, this definition goes very much wider than definitions of racially motivated *crime*. Not only is it difficult to use for comparison with figures for such crime from other countries, but it is often misunderstood within Britain. For example, some incidents involve quite young children harassing a person from a minority group; as they are below the age of criminal responsibility there can be no prosecution. In others, say a brawl between individuals from two ethnic minority groups, a police officer may infer a racial motivation when it does not apply to that incident in fact. And allegations of racial motivation may not always be well-founded. The pilot study comments:

> Care must be exercised when publishing information about racial incidents. Of the 163 Racial Incident Reports (RIR) recorded throughout Thames Valley in 1993, only five led to prosecutions. This is not intended as a criticism of the police, but the clear-up rate could be a source of apprehension among minority groups and contribute to a possible continuance of under-reporting of racially motivated crime to the police. Ethnic minority confidence in the policing of racially motivated crime might be enhanced if an explanation of the statistical information could be given.

Many of the reported incidents, though unpleasant, were not unlawful.

A detailed examination of the RIR data reveals the following:

●  105 of the 163 recorded incidents involved criminal activities, but these included at least 11 where no racial motivation was apparent, even though one or more of the parties was of ethnic minority origin.

●  In the remaining 58 incidents, no crime appeared to have been committed. These incidents could more properly be described as tension indicators, and although clearly of strategic importance to the Thames Valley Police, they do not constitute racially motivated crime.

●  The RIR form, correctly, permits the victim, the recording officer, and any third party to record their belief about whether the incident was racially motivated. Disagreement occurred in some cases. It was significant that in at least five cases the police officer regarded the crime as racially motivated, whereas the victim did not. Although the judgement of the police officer might ultimately have been proved to be incorrect, it nevertheless suggested an awareness among police officers of particular patterns of crimes where racial motivation might have been a factor.

- Only three cases made mention of referral to Victim Support. This is almost certainly a consequence of the policy of Thames Valley Police *automatically* to refer all cases to Victim Support where victims are personally aggrieved. Indeed this opinion was corroborated by Victim Support staff who stated that in all but the most serious crimes, where the consent of the victim was required, referrals were always instituted.

- Eleven of the RIR cases involved children, as perpetrators, under the age of criminal responsibility. This was a surprisingly low proportion, because the police and other agencies believe that children account for a significantly high level of racially motivated behaviour. The apparent underrepresentation might be a consequence of the police dealing more informally with young people.

- The police consider that a significant number of cases involving minors are provoked by parents or peer groups. In all but three of the 11 cases involving minors the police spoke to their parents, advising them of the anti-social nature of such activities.

- In eight out of 152 RIRs, the police noted that the local authority Housing Department would be notified of the incident. In seven of these, the referrals were in relation to the welfare of the victim.

- Eight of the RIRs stated that the incident had occurred in or around school premises, and that police officers had notified the schools directly. None of these cases appeared to involve the use of the criminal law. Each of them was concerned with differing levels of harassment, and the informal approach to the problem by the police suggests that, in some cases, their reluctance to invoke the criminal law was due to the age of those concerned, rather than the nature of the possible crime committed.

The decision whether or not to prosecute for crime has since 1986 rested with a separate Crown Prosecution Service (CPS); before then, the police themselves took the decision. The Oxford study found that many among the ethnic minorities were probably unaware of this change, and might still blame the police for a failure to prosecute.

Since 1 April 1995, the CPS has been monitoring racially motivated crimes, but as its system relates only to *charges* brought by the police, it does not deal with all the racial incidents that may be reported. The monitoring system analyses the reasons for CPS decisions – whether to proceed with a case or drop it; records whether racial motivation was brought specifically to the court's attention; and whether or not the court specifically referred to racial motivation as an exacerbating feature. The CPS does not monitor the ethnicity of defendants. At the time of the pilot study, the Severn/Thames area of the CPS was dealing with 26,000 cases (of all kinds) in a year, and considered such monitoring to be too heavy a burden on its resources. However, the CPS nationally is considering full ethnic monitoring of defendants.

Underlying this pilot study are repeated references to distrust and suspicion of the police among ethnic minorities. Victim Support, a national, publicly-funded agency directed to assisting victims of every kind of crime, is said to have met difficulties in its attempts to recruit voluntary helpers from among the minorities because its close association with the police may be regarded with suspicion. Victim Support has recently increased its efforts to help victims of racially motivated crime, and uses nationally agreed categories for ethnic monitoring in recording its work, though adding to these from its own list to include Cypriot, Irish, Jewish and Gypsy victims.

It is worth emphasising here that ethnic monitoring is used in Britain as a means of trying to identify discrimination and promote racial equality. The nationally agreed list of categories is compiled and recommended by the CRE, and was used by the government to devise an 'ethnic question' in the Census for the first time in 1991. The agreed list (to which the CRE itself recently added 'Irish') reads:

| | |
|---|---|
| White | Indian |
| Black - African | Pakistani |
| Black - Caribbean | Bangladeshi |
| Black - Other (please specify) | Chinese |
| Other (please specify) | |

Many public and private concerns in Britain have adopted ethnic monitoring in order to check on equal opportunity in employment or access to services. But obviously the categories used are not all easily transferable for use in other countries. The Netherlands, for example, has a list of its own while France absolutely refuses to have one at all. These differences of approach cast an interesting light on attempts to compare different concepts of racially motivated crime.

The recommended multi-agency approach was adopted in Oxfordshire in 1991 and is considered by the agencies involved to be an effective vehicle for tackling racially motivated crime. It includes City and County Council officers from Housing, Education and Social Services Departments, the Probation Service, Severn Thames Crown Prosecution Service, Thames Valley Police and Oxfordshire Victim Support.

This brief summary of the pilot study in Oxfordshire is not intended to give a proper estimation of the situation there or the response to it, but to indicate the kind of framework a British researcher is likely to use when beginning a study of responses to racially motivated crime. It provides some measure of comparison with the contrasting approaches in Frankfurt, Lyons and Rome, which together form Chapters Two to Four of this publication. Chapter Five suggests how the work, as a whole, might be used to improve cooperation on this problem at European level.

### Recent developments

Racial incidents recorded by the police both nationally and within individual police areas have continued to increase. For example in the Thames Valley area, reported racial incidents rose from 233 in 1994/95 to 266 in 1995/96. Underreporting of racial incidents also persists, with recent surveys in the London area ( the British Crime Survey and the survey by the Policy Studies Institute) suggesting that reported racial incidents represent, at best, 50% of all such incidents. There are also variations in the levels of reporting by different racial groups.

As racial incidents grew and received greater publicity, so did the demand for more effective legislation. In 1994, when the Criminal Justice and Public Order Bill was being debated in Parliament, the Government resisted demands to create a separate criminal offence of racial harassment. Instead, a new offence of 'intentional harassment', which has no racial element, was added as section 4A of the Public Order Act 1986. This new section came into force in February 1995. Most indications are that it is rarely used, primarily because of the need to prove 'intention' as well as the offending conduct and the resultant harassment, alarm or distress.

A 'stalking bill', which reached the statute books as the Protection from Harassment Act 1997, created a criminal offence of harassment and an offence of causing fear of violence which could be utilised to arrest and prosecute where harassment or threats are racially motivated. A novel feature of the 1997 Act is the ability of the trial court to impose a restraining order (comparable to conditions of bail), breach of which is a fresh offence carrying up to five years' impriconment. The 1997 Act also enables civil injunctions to prevent recurrence of harassment, with criminal sanctions for any breach.

While Parliament has not directly tackled racial violence, the Court of Appeal has done so in respect of sentencing when it ruled, in *R v Ribbans*, that a proven racial element in an offence of violence is a gravely aggravating feature justifying an increase in sentence.

Following the general election in May 1997 the new Labour Government committed itself, in its first Parliamentary session, to create new criminal offences of racially motivated violence and racial harassment which are likely to carry heavier tariffs than the existing offences without race as a factor. These new offences will form part of a Crime and Disorder Bill which will be introduced in about November 1997. The impact of the law depends, of course, on those involved in its enforcement. New, or existing, criminal offences will only be effective in  punishing and deterring racially motivated crime if the police are sufficiently committed to this objective. Similarly, the *Ribbans* ruling will influence sentencing in future cases only to the extent that the police and the Crown Prosecution Service bring evidence of racial motivation to the attention of the court.

Alongside developments in the criminal justice system has been the growing role of local authorities, in their capacity as landlords, in the prevention of racially motivated crime. Local authorities are gradually recognising their responsibility and their legal powers to take action in relation to racial incidents on their housing estates. During the 12 months uptil May 1996, local authorities in London succeeded in evicting or obtaining injunctions against tenants who had racially harassed their neighbours in over 60 cases. In the Housing Act 1996, Parliament has strengthened the hands of all residential landlords with a new statutory ground for eviction which encompasses racial harassment; this Act also gives local authorities a power to protect their tenants and their visitors from repeated harassment by means of an injunction where violence has been used or threatened. The Crime and Disorder Bill is expected to expand the use of civil orders to restrain criminal behaviour.

## THE GERMAN BACKGROUND

Wide publicity for racial violence in Germany since 1991 has produced some predictable but often erroneous reactions. Some people (including some Germans) believe that racial violence is more common in East Germany than in West Germany, and explain this simplistically in terms of a reaction against a communist past or economic difficulties in the east. In fact racial violence is statistically as likely in the west as in the east. Others fear a resurgence of Nazi political power. While the seriousness of a threat to society from neo-Nazi movements should not be underestimated, Germany is far from unique in having active neo-Nazi groups – these exist in many European countries – whereas Germany is unique in the determination of its government and the majority of its population never again to allow its past, from 1933 to 1945, to be repeated. Racial violence is taken very seriously. One small example of this was that the foreign affairs minister attended the funeral of the Turkish family killed by an arson attack in Mölln in 1993. Even so there were some angry comments that the Chancellor himself should have attended. (There has never been any question of a British home secretary or prime minister attending a funeral in similar circumstances.)

It is, therefore, not surprising that the report on Frankfurt describes a carefully organised and detailed set of responses to racial violence in that city. The author, Anjana Das, concludes that, despite the weaknesses which her report uncovers,

> ... the combination of a strong political commitment to combating racially motivated crime with the implementation of anti-racist policies has produced some effective countermeasures.

And she points out that the Kahn Committee, a body set up by the European Community in June 1994 to produce a Community-wide strategy against racism and xenophobia, commended the good conduct of Frankfurt's judicial agencies and included many recommendations for action which were already being implemented in that city.

This is not to say, of course, that everything in Frankfurt is perfect. A fundamental problem everywhere in combating racially motivated crime is the difficulty of obtaining accurate and sufficient knowledge of its extent. Victims often fail to report it. Official records may not describe adequately even those incidents which are reported. Then there is a time factor; an apparent increase in racially motivated crime may reflect increased diligence in tracking it down rather than an actual increase in its perpetration. But in a place like Frankfurt, where great efforts are being made, one can at least see the problems of combating such crime much more clearly than in places where it is not taken seriously. And this fact, in turn, leads towards suggestions for new answers.

We know most about racial violence in places where the most is being done to combat it. In Germany, the *Land* of Berlin is very active in anti-racist work, largely thanks to the work of Barbara John of the Senate's *Ausländerbeauftragte*. But the position varies greatly between one *Land* and another. Germany has a very decentralised government, partly for historical reasons dating back long before the present century, and formally because of the provisions of the Basic Law adopted after the Second World War. Each *Land* has considerable law-making and administrative powers. What happens in Hesse, where Frankfurt is the capital, can be very different from what happens in Saxony or Bavaria. Some *Länder*, for example, have laws against sex discrimination, others do not. Each *Land* has its own rules and procedures on the reception of refugees. The terms for naturalisation as a German citizen are laid down in federal law but administered by the *Land* authorities. These are just some of the reasons why the situation in Frankfurt should not be taken as typical of all Germany. Other reasons are given in the report.

Germany is a country which only formally came into existence as a nation state in 1871. The borders of the small states of which it was composed had fluctuated over the centuries, now including and now excluding people of Polish, French, Danish and other origins. Yet modern German citizenship is rooted in a myth of ethnic German-ness, so strong that it includes people of German descent from other countries and rejects the idea that anyone from outside can easily or fully become German. Until very recently, Germans firmly believed their country was not a country of immigration, even though millions of immigrants have arrived in the twentieth century.

Immigration has been either encouraged, or at least permitted, over a long period for strictly economic reasons, theoretically as a series of temporary measures to admit workers who were not going to remain. Even though many have in fact stayed permanently, they have remained foreigners both under the law (which does not grant citizenship by birth on German territory but only by descent from a German parent) and in general perception. In this way, children born in Germany to parents themselves born in Germany to Turkish immigrants are still counted and regarded as Turks. But even European Community nationals from southern and eastern Europe, although they enjoy all the rights and benefits of Community nationals to live and work in Germany, are seen as outsiders. And all outsiders are targets for the young right-wing extremists who believe fanatically in Germany for the Germans. Thus racial attacks in Germany are perceived as attacks on foreigners. Poles and Italians may be as much at risk as Turks and black Africans. However, the attacks are racial in a more widely accepted sense, in that a black German citizen or a naturalised Turk is also at risk; whatever their legal status they are still regarded as outsiders, as not really German, by the extreme right.

The reunification of Germany in 1990 created new pressures. Many workers from the east were eager to move westwards once they had the chance, and their labour threatened the position of immigrant workers in the west. The German government took measures to discourage this westward movement, wishing to invest in, and maintain some stability in, the east. West Germans soon developed a superior attitude to the eastern compatriots they had so long sought to be reunited with – the easterners looked poor, they talked differently, their attitudes seemed primitive. With the more general opening of borders to the east, people of German descent from the old Soviet Union, Romania and other countries seized their chance to move westwards and claim German citizenship. All these migrants, being legally German, are left out of immigration figures, but several million of them moved into West Germany and Berlin in a few years, creating a large demand for jobs, housing and services which the German government coped with remarkably well. But now a pecking-order appeared: West Germans at the top, then easterners, then 'German' immigrants from other countries, who often appeared much more foreign than German, and finally the foreign immigrants already present (including some African and Vietnamese immigrants in the east).

It must be emphasised that Germany has had a settled population of non-EC immigrants for a long time. The term 'guest-workers', used for Turks and others in the 1960s and after, reflected the official theory that workers were being admitted temporarily only and for strictly economic reasons. But with time, families have arrived and some security of residence has been given to those who at first had only temporary permission to remain. There are now 5.9 million foreigners resident in Germany (including some EC nationals) in a total population of about 80 million.

Meanwhile, asylum seekers from many countries were also using the newly opened borders to reach Germany and add to the number of new arrivals. It was in this context that the outbreaks of racial violence from 1991 onwards occurred. There had already been a mounting campaign against refugees throughout the 1980s. Germany's Basic Law had included provision for free entry for asylum seekers, and this was eventually amended in 1993. But still they came, many impelled by the civil war in Yugoslavia, others from much farther afield, in Asia and Africa, coming through east European countries to try their chance in Germany. In recent years, German controls on immigration and asylum have been tightened, although not nearly so severely as those of France or Britain.

In Britain, where many opinion-formers still seem to be obsessed by anti-German feelings from fifty years ago and earlier, there is usually little appreciation of modern Germany's anxiety for peace and for the maintenance of a democracy where power is widely distributed. There was strong public reaction against the violent attacks on refugees, Gypsies and Turks in Hoyerswerda, Rostock, Mölln and elsewhere; hundreds of thousands of anti-racist demonstrators took to the streets. One may be able to learn more from the similarities between perpetrators of racial violence in different countries in the present than from comparisons with the last days of the Weimar Republic. This is not to say that the past does not matter; in all countries appeals to the past are important politically and emotionally. It is the character and accuracy of interpretations of the past that matter.

## THE FRENCH BACKGROUND

In the last half-century Lyons has become one of the foremost cities of France, ambitious for an international role and a metropolitan character. New motorways, skyscrapers and other grand buildings, and a significant increase in population have transformed it into an image of twentieth century commercial prosperity. But in France, a heavily centralised country, decisions taken in Paris still count for much. The Prefects, who are responsible for policing their regions or departments, are appointed by, and responsible to, the Ministry of the Interior.

During the Second World War Lyons was a centre of French resistance, after the country had been divided between the German-occupied north, including Paris, and the territory of the Vichy government in the south. It was also the centre of operations of the notorious Nazi, Klaus Barbie, the 'butcher of Lyons'. This experience left a deeply polarised population and many bitter memories. Many Jews were sent to their deaths from Vichy France, with the active cooperation of some police officers, many of whom remained in post after the war.

The wartime experience produced deep suspicions of ethnic monitoring among the very anti-racists who today might be expected to ask for it. In 1940/1 an ethnic census collected information that was used to identify Jews in a series of police raids. It is now an offence under French data protection legislation to keep ethnic records. The National Employment Agency (ANPE) has several times been prosecuted for using them, not for benevolent purposes, but to assist in acts of discrimination.[5] The background is therefore quite different from that in Britain and the United States. Ethnic monitoring in France is perceived as racist by anti-racists. One might compare this difference with the issue of school bussing in Britain and the United States in the 1960s. Black Americans demanded bussing to overcome the segregation in schools that had resulted from segregated housing patterns. In Britain, the government wanted to bus black children away from predominantly black schools, but was strongly opposed by black activists who objected to their children being transported many miles from home. Policies with apparently similar names and purposes met diametrically opposite reactions. This is a useful illustration of the need for caution in transferring policies from one country to another.

---

5. See *Libération*, 13 January 1995.

The political background to racial issues in France is very different from that in most other European countries. Broadly speaking, both left and centre-right take for granted a theory of the nation rooted in Enlightenment values:

> An intolerance of other cultures is expressed in the name of the progressive and ratio-nalist values associated with the 1789 revolution ... For those whose cultural frame of reference was formed by the Enlightenment, other cultures with a different reference point were inevitably seen as backward and lower down the scale of human progress.[6]

The extreme right may make its appeal to a point further back in history: Catholic France's fight against Islam, for example. But this, combined with the fierce secularism of many in the moderate and far left, has resulted in widespread hostility to Islam and, by association, to Muslim immigrants from north Africa. There are additional reasons for hostility to Algerians in particular. The Algerian war of independence in the 1950s was traumatic for the French. French colonialism, on the other hand, rouses bitter memories among Algerians and also Moroccans, Tunisians and Vietnamese (all of them represented among the present immigrant population of Lyons).

French colonialism sought to make its colonial citizens as French as pos-sible, believing French culture and a French outlook to be the greatest gift that could be bestowed. Colour and ethnic origin were in this context sup-posed to be irrelevant. Therefore, many French people firmly believe that racism is not a term applicable to their society. Indeed it is not lawful in France to categorise people as members of racial groups or ethnic minorities for any official purpose, making effective ethnic monitoring impossible and discussion of racially motivated crime exceedingly difficult. Colette Smith suggests that the categories used elsewhere for such crime simply cannot be applied to France. Yet in reality racially motivated crime is directed in France against people from north Africa of Maghrébin ((that is Tunisian, Moroccan or Algerian) appearance, whether they are French citizens or not; against other visibly different foreigners; and also against Jews. Anywhere else, there would be little difficulty about using the word 'racial' in this context, but in France the term is usually avoided. On the side of the immigrants them-selves, however, there is less reserve, although the term is used more selec-tively than in Britain.

This is not to say that the French approve of racism. They find it abhor-rent. But their definition of it emphasises racist utterances more than actions. French anti-racist statements frequently include a denunciation of denials that the Nazi holocaust of Jews ever took place. The anti-racist law gives much space to racist speech and writing. However, its provisions dealing with everyday discrimination in employment have hardly been imple-mented. And, as the Lyons report shows, there is no special offence of racial violence, no concept of racial harassment in public housing, and no explicit guidance to schools on racial incidents. Support for the victims of racially motivated crime is limited to the activities, not systematically organised as

---

6. Cathie Lloyd and Hazel Waters, 'France: One culture, one people?', *Race and Class*, 32, No. 3, 1991.

such, of the churches and of voluntary associations.

An important feature of this difference of approach is that one cannot usefully compare the figures published by the Consultative Commission for Human Rights (based in the French Prime Minister's office), and quoted briefly by Colette Smith in her report on Lyons, with figures from other countries. These figures, compiled by official information services rely essentially upon police estimates of the character of an attack or threat. The Commission lists in its latest report for the whole of metropolitan France in 1995 only 23 racist acts, including nine woundings and seven killings. Racist threats in France are said to have numbered 445 in 1995. (Figures for Corsica are compiled separately.) The examples of attackers refer to people associated with the extreme right, who themselves give racist reasons for their actions. The Commission comments that, on the other hand, a soldier marked with the blood of a north African who was found dead in Bayonne, riddled with bullets, was found guilty of murder, but the incident was not recorded as a racial attack because the enquiry could not determine the real motives of the killer.[7] With so strict a definition of racial incidents one may reasonably suppose that official figures seriously underestimate the problem. Colette Smith's interviews with members of the legal profession support this supposition: even the cases which get to a court may not feature in the statistics, and she describes how difficult it is, even with the help of an association, to bring cases to court at all. The Consultative Commission itself has repeatedly asked the Ministry of the Interior to revise its statistical methods.

The Lyons report includes a description of local associations of various kinds. An association has legal status in France. If it registers legally, it is entitled to certain benefits such as tax rebates and funding from local authorities. In 1939 a law was passed forbidding foreigners to control or lead an association, the motive at the time being to exclude fascist groups. After the war, many associations which included foreigners therefore had French people nominally at their head. In 1981 the Mitterrand government repealed the 1939 law, making it much easier for foreigners to form and belong to associations. However, much of the expansion which then took place was due to greater availability of funding.

An issue of great concern to minorities in France, and one entwined with incidents of racial violence, has long been the bad housing of immigrants. Immigrant hostels have often been targets for arson by the extreme right. In the Lyons suburb of Vaulx en Velin there were riots in 1981, partly in protest against police harassment of young people and partly over bad housing, and the city then made great efforts to improve the area. But in 1990 there were more riots there, when an immigrant pillion passenger on a motor-cycle was killed (locals believed deliberately) by a police car.

In both France and Italy the issue of racial violence is closely intertwined with the question of immigration law. In both countries, for quite different

---

7. Commission Nationale Consultative des Droits de L'Homme (1996): *La Lutte contre le Racisme et la Xénophobie: Exclusion et Droits de L'Homme*, La documentation française, 1996, pp 21-32.

reasons, illegal immigration was tolerated in practice for a long time: in France because employers needed cheap and flexible immigrant labour, and could not get enough of it through the official schemes for admitting migrant workers; and in Italy because of a generally casual attitude towards rules and regulations, coupled with the fact that nobody was making immigration a political issue before the late 1980s. The Italian immigration debate is described in the report on Rome. The extreme right there has chosen to make immigration a major issue and to encourage hostility towards immigrants. In France, a clamp-down on immigration began earlier, in the 1970s, when France, like many other countries, was suffering from an economic downturn. In 1972 the government introduced new immigration controls and, at the same time, accepted an anti-racist law proposed by the opposition. In 1973 there was an outburst of racial violence, spreading over several months from Marseilles to other parts of France, and directed mainly against Algerians. By 1974 the extreme right group, Ordre Nouveau, was campaigning against illegal immigrants as a danger to France, culturally and economically. (Ordre Nouveau set up the National Front in 1972 as its parliamentary wing.) The Bonnet Law of 1980 made it easier for the authorities to deport illegal immigrants. A brief liberalisation of controls when Mitterrand first came to power was followed by the rapid rise of the French National Front from 1983 onwards in electoral politics. Fear of the National Front impelled governments to become ever more restrictive, resulting in the Pasqua laws of 1986 and 1993. It is to these that Colette Smith refers when she mentions the 'Pasqua effect' in Lyons.

Indeed it is a striking feature of the Lyons report that the respondents in interviews always speak, whatever the terms of the questions put to them, about security of residence and fear of removal from France. One would expect that questions about racially motivated crime would produce examples of incidents similar to those found in Britain, Germany and Italy. But in Lyons the framework of perception seems to be very different. The main threat to physical security is perceived to be seizure and removal from the country by the police and, associated with this, violence on the part of the police. The Maghrébins under threat do not expect any redress, for the police are only implementing policies determined by the state authorities themselves.

The impetus for strict controls does not come only from the extreme right. For a long time the received view among senior French officials has been that a 'threshold of tolerance' exists and that any given society can absorb no more than a certain maximum number of 'strangers'. Exceeding this maximum would lead to social conflict.[8] Racist violence would follow unless the numbers were reduced.

To understand how serious is the insecurity felt by people of Maghrébin descent, one must appreciate the depth of their uncertainty about their legal status, and also their vulnerability to purely administrative procedures where discretion plays a large part. The basic French immigration law of 1945 has

8. See Rob Witte, *Racist Violence and the State: A comparative European analysis*, doctoral thesis, Utrecht, 1995 .

been amended over and over again: first tightened, then liberalised to some extent, then tightened again. The first Pasqua law, in September 1986, conferred on Prefects, acting alone and without the requirement of any procedure whereby a defence could be heard, the power to enforce the escort of an illegal immigrant to the frontier; it re-established rules on expulsion which had been suspended in 1981; and it reduced the categories of foreigners protected against removal and increased the number of documents required for entry into French territory. Some but not all of these measures were liberalised by the Joxe law of 1989.

Further Pasqua laws in 1993 introduced new controls, including sanctions on carrying companies, the withdrawal of a right to work for asylum seekers and the creation of 'waiting zones' for detention in ports and airports. There were also significant changes to rules on residence, benefits and family reunion. The almost automatic right to remain of a person who had come to live in France as a child after reaching the age of majority was withdrawn. A person whose status was in any way irregular (for example not having filed the right documents at the right time) immediately lost the right to benefit, even if he or she had worked and contributed to national insurance for several years. Officially, these measures were to protect national security. The French lawyers' organisation GISTI (Groupe d'Information et de Soutien aux Travailleurs Immigrés) has commented that they neither improved security nor reduced the number of illegal migrants – the measure as a whole actually transformed many legal residents into 'illegals'. GISTI further accuses the French government of promoting racism and xenophobia by the Pasqua laws, and of creating insecurity and exclusion among the minorities whom it claimed to want to integrate. Also, under cover of battling against illegal migration, the government was encouraging informers in every part of the public administration to denounce individuals.[9]

The complexity of the law, its severity, and the lack of procedural protections are frightening for those who are uncertain of their status, and such people do not approach the police for guidance for obvious reasons. Moreover, despite the protection which in theory exists under the anti-racist law of 1972 against the 'racially motivated crime' of unjust discrimination, the victims of discrimination know all too well, as the Lyons report brings out, that they have little hope of bringing a successful case – besides, they can do so only by complaining to the police, and fear of the police stands in the way of doing that. Many residents of immigrant origin are now uncertain whether they are French citizens or not, because yet another Pasqua law, that of July 1993, altered the rules of acquisition, in part with retrospective effect. It is bad enough for people to discover they are not citizens when they had so far been treated as such, but even worse is the uncertainty among many who may or may not be citizens but who dare not enquire for fear of possible removal. It is no wonder that the Pasqua laws play such a large part in the Lyons interviews.

---

9. GISTI, *Les Guides de l'entrée et du séjour des étrangers en France*, Edition La Découverte, Paris 1995.

## THE ITALIAN BACKGROUND

While France and Germany have, at varying periods in the twentieth century, encouraged the immigration of workers for economic reasons, Italian governments have never done so. Italy, in this century, has been a country of emigration. Millions of Italians have left, some permanently and some temporarily, to go to the United States, Australia, Latin America, Germany, France, Belgium, the United Kingdom and elsewhere. With the rapid economic growth of northern Italy during years of increasing prosperity after the Second World War, there has also been large scale internal migration from the south to the industrial north. Go to Sicily in August and you will hear the accents of New Jersey and Sydney, see suitcases from Frankfurt and London, and meet uncles and cousins from Turin and Bologna, all home to visit the all-important family for a few weeks. In the 1970s, when there were demonstrations against immigration in some northern countries, there were demonstrations in southern Italy demanding 'No more emigration'.

A few African faces had long been familiar, mostly from Italy's former colonies. There was little evidence of racism in Italy before the 1980s. Racism had never been central to the doctrines of Italian fascism as it was to German Nazism, though anti-semitism became an increasingly important part of Mussolini's policy from the late 1930s onwards. Fascism exalted state power and romanticised violence. Violence was a noble, purifying force in theory; in practice it was used, through the organisation of blackshirt gangs, to beat up opponents. Nationalism and militarism were held to be glorious. The chief opponents of fascism in the 1920s and 1930s were the communists, a group to which many of the intelligentsia belonged and continued to belong in the post-war years.

After the Second World War fascism was utterly discredited. But fascists had been in power since 1922, and numerous officials, teachers, police officers and others, appointed under that regime and still sympathetic to it, retained their posts. Although the Communist Party commanded considerable support, it never held power. The United States government, anxious to back any kind of anti-communism, supported the Christian Democrats, as did the Vatican. From 1945 to 1981, there was always a Christian Democrat prime minister, leading a coalition dominated by his own party. Meanwhile, only a relatively small party, the Movimento Sociale Italiano (MSI), was advocating fascist policies.

Racial violence in Italy today has to be seen against the background of Italian politics. Governments were unstable, often lasting less than a year. The administration was riddled with corruption. Organised crime, particularly on the part of the Mafia, grew enormously in the post-war decades, reaching Rome and Milan, and allegedly involving Giuliano Andreotti himself, who was many times prime minister. The Mafia committed hundreds of murders a year, killing, among others, honest judges, officials and journalists as well as criminal rivals. It has emerged recently that both the Christian Democrat and Socialist parties were largely financed by crime. Bribery and protection money were an everyday part of dealings of all sorts, from public contracts to the operations of private firms, large and small. The majority of the Italian population has suffered from the effects of this corruption; many of them have shown great courage in standing up to it, and others have been terrorised into active connivance with crime.

Apart from acts of criminal violence, for at least thirty years there have been acts of political violence by extremists on both the right and the left. There was much publicity for the atrocities of the left-wing Red Brigades. The authorities were, however, less zealous in pursuing the perpetrators of right-wing terrorism, such as the bomb attacks on a bank in Milan in 1969 which killed 17 people and injured 88; the bombing in 1974 in Brescia of a trade union meeting, killing eight; and the worst single outrage, the bombing of Bologna railway station which killed 85 and injured 200 people. It was shown that secret service agents had been active in obstructing the investigations. Some members of MSI have been implicated in acts of violence.

Partly because of political instability, but mainly because of corruption, Italian public services are disorganised and often close to breakdown. The honest and conscientious civil servants, police officers and other officials have to struggle with impossible situations, lacking resources and often remaining unpaid themselves for months on end. Such is the vitality and resilience of the country that somehow most things keep running most of the time, and the foreign tourist may hardly be aware of the huge, underlying problems. But implementation of the law obviously suffers. As the report on Rome shows, the application of immigration law, anti-racist law and laws on violence is deeply flawed. But so too is the implementation of numerous other laws.

Even though the full extent of corruption was not yet public knowledge, the population generally was becoming deeply disillusioned with politicians from 1979 onwards, and both major parties – Christian Democrat and Communist – began to lose electoral support. From 1983 onwards, the Communist Party began to soften its line, becoming more like a centre-left party than a Marxist one. At the same time, it continued to attack the corrupt practices and connivance with the Mafia that had kept a combination of Christian Democrats and Socialists in power. After the fall of communist régimes in eastern Europe in 1989, the Italian Communist Party dissolved, and most of its members re-formed as the Democratic Party of the Left (PDS). The whole political scene changed. Fear of communism could no longer be exploited in order to keep existing rulers in power, and smaller parties gained. The country in the early 1990s was split three ways: between the north, where the Northern League made rapid gains; the centre, still a bastion of the left; and the south, where the MSI greatly increased its support.

The Northern League, led by Umberto Bossi, was driven by a hatred of the south, which was accused of being the source of all corruption and also, because of its poverty and because it received large-scale aid, a drain on the wealth of the north. The League was also hostile to the central government, and wanted either a federal state or outright secession of the northern regions. Bossi's hostility was directed at first against southerners, but when immigration became a national issue he also attacked immigration from Africa.

The MSI was a mixture of open fascism and covert fascism under a moderate guise. Unlike the League, it strongly upheld centralised state power. But it was also hostile to immigrants from Asia and Africa. Its leader, Gianfranco Fini, at first proclaimed himself a moderate, but in October 1992 his followers celebrated the fiftieth anniversary of Mussolini's march on Rome with black shirts and Roman salutes. Fini himself repeatedly referred to Mussolini as the greatest world statesman of the century.

After the general election of 1992, the new prime minister, Giuliano Amato, a Socialist presiding over a Socialist-Christian Democrat coalition, set in motion a major attack on corruption in public life. Magistrates uncovered the story of how ministers, senior civil servants and businessmen had been enriching themselves at the public expense. The Ferruzzi agro-industrial empire, for example, had paid US$90 million to political parties just before the election in return for promises of state help. In Sicily, other magistrates were continuing the work of Giovanni Falcone, assassinated by the Mafia because of his investigations. One of the new investigators, Paolo Borsellino, was assassinated together with five of his police guards. Evidence emerged of informers within the police service. Seven thousand soldiers were despatched to Sicily, and favourable treatment was offered to mafiosi who were willing to break their law of silence and give evidence in court. So began a series of startling revelations about major politicians. A former prime minister, the Socialist Bettino Craxi, was interrogated on 170 counts of misbehaviour. He later fled to Tunisia. Three other former prime ministers, Giuliano Andreotti, Giovanni Forlani and Arnaldo Goria, were warned that they were under police investigation. Several senior judges and ambassadors were suspended or arrested.

Local elections in 1993 resulted in a strong shift away from the Christian Democrat and Socialist parties to the League in the north and the MSI in the south. In 1994 a disillusioned electorate turned to a man who had never been a party politician, Silvio Berlusconi. One of the richest men in Europe, he ran a vast financial empire which included major television stations. He formed his own party, Forza Italia, only weeks before the election. His success in becoming prime minister was owed to his skill in reaching a pact with the Northern League and the MSI to form a National Alliance (Alleanza Nazionale). By agreeing not to compete with each other, the three parties gained a majority in the Lower House of Parliament. Berlusconi's promises to reduce taxes and create a million new jobs were not kept. Within months he had lost popular support, and the magistrates in Milan had disclosed that Berlusconi's own company, Fininvest, was under official investigation for corruption. Berlusconi himself was committed for trial in October 1995.

One result of all these events was that the courts simply could not cope with all the criminal proceedings being instituted. Delays are still hampering the emergence of the full facts about years of corruption. Obviously there have been many indirect effects upon society as a whole and upon the racial situation. Italy's economy has suffered severely from corruption. Attempts by the Amato government to reduce public expenditure got rid of some abuses but also hit many poorer people. Unemployment, as elsewhere in Europe, has grown over recent years. It was into this volatile situation that African and Asian immigrants entered during the 1980s and early 1990s. Their entry and stay were for the most part unregulated. Many took work unofficially, just as many Italians had for years been taking work unofficially, in the so-called 'black economy', with neither employers nor employees paying taxes or national insurance.

It is, in practice, impossible to distinguish illegal immigrants from asylum seekers in Italy. Very few people try to apply for asylum because the chances of acceptance are so low, and because flight from civil war or starvation does not qualify for refugee status under the Geneva Convention. But many Africans have come as fugitives from terrible situations, while others, impelled by poverty, have hoped to earn a living in Europe. For some, Italy was not the intended destination but merely the easiest country to enter by sea across the Mediterranean on the way to Germany – which they never reached.

Those who got stuck in the south found themselves in a largely rural region with high unemployment, and managed to survive by doing low-paid day labour in the fields, or casual work in the catering trade, or begging. Some were recruited by criminal organisations. Others penetrated to northern cities, where they encountered the conditions described in the Rome report.

Voluntary organisations, many of them sponsored by the Catholic church, have struggled to help the immigrants. Doctors and nurses have often given their services free. One should not underestimate the humanitarian and anti-racist traditions in Italy that exist side by side with hostility and racial violence. But the great wave of immigration in the 1980s and 1990s has been too much for the resources available. Estimates of the illegal immigrant population at the end of the 1980s varied between half a million and one million. Moreover, in addition to the Africans and Asians, East Europeans have been entering since 1989. There was a great public outcry against the authorities when the government decided to turn back thousands of Albanians in 1993. But others have entered, notably from Bosnia. Also, many Gypsies from East European countries have arrived, and prejudice against Gypsies already existed. According to former parliamentarian, Laura Balbo,[10] Italy has altered in the last few years from a country where some racism existed into a racist society (*una società di ordinario razzismo*).

The section on Rome reports incidents and cases from other places in Italy as well as in the region of the capital itself. Given the difficulty, vividly painted in the report, of obtaining reliable statistics and coherent information on racially motivated crime in Rome, this method helps to build up a general picture, showing the importance of the party political background at any one time and illustrating the mobility of the right-wing groups, whose demonstrations and organised bands of attackers have had a great impact in the 1990s.

Research for this report was done, and the report written, in 1995, and Italy's political scene has changed again between its completion and its publication. In April 1996 a new centre-left coalition named L'Olive won a general election. Jolanda Chirico's use of the present tense in describing the

---

10. Laura Balbo and Luigi Manconi, *I Razzismi Reali*, Feltrinelli, Milan 1992.

immediate political background should therefore be understood to refer to the period of her research. The situation she analyses has not changed fundamentally, but the volatility of Italian politics is such that it might have changed radically by the time these words are printed. Umberto Bossi's threat to make northern Italy secede from the nation, coupled as it is with strongly racist propaganda, will surely leave harmful effects behind it, whether it succeeds or fails.

This brief sketch cannot describe the Italian situation adequately, but one point must be added: the lenient sentencing policies which Jolanda Chirico describes are not unique to cases of racially motivated crime. Many convicted individuals never go to prison. This hardly excuses the treatment of racial violence by the authorities, but it is a part of the context which must be understood.

## References

Balbo, Laura and Luigi Manconi, *I Razzismi Reali*, Feltrinelli, Milan 1992.

Commission Nationale Consultative des Droits de L'Homme, *La Lutte contre le Racisme et la Xénophobie: Exclusion et Droits de L'Homme*, La documentation française, 1996.

GISTI, *Les Guides de l'Entrée et du Séjour des Etrangers en France*, Editions La Découverte, Paris 1995.

Jaffrey, Marc and Jonathan Stanley, *Tackling Racial Harassment: A caseworkers's handbook*, Commission for Racial Equality, London, 1995.

Lloyd, Cathie and Hazel Waters, 'France: One culture, one people?' *Race and Class*, 32, No 3, 1991.

*Racial Violence and Harassment in Europe*, Consultant's Report for the Council of Europe Community Relations Project, London, June 1991.

*Racially Motivated Crime: A British Crime Survey Analysis*, Home Office Research and Planning Unit, Paper 82, London 1994.

Simons, Barry, *Revised Racial Harassment Procedures (Public and Private Sectors)*, London Borough of Newham, 1991.

*Taking Steps: Multi-agency responses to racial attacks and harassment*, Home Office, London 1996.

*The Response to Racial Attacks and Harassment: Guidance for the statutory agencies*, Report of the Inter-Departmental Racial Attacks Group, Home Office, London, 1989.

Witte, Rob, *Racist Violence and the State: A comparative European analysis*, doctoral thesis, Utrecht, 1995.

*CHAPTER  TWO*

# FRANKFURT

Anjana Das

## RACIALLY MOTIVATED CRIME IN GERMANY

### The extent of the problem

Since 1991 the number of racially motivated attacks has risen significantly throughout Germany. That year there was a highly emotional national discussion concerning the law on asylum and the influx of refugees into Germany. It was within that heated political climate that the horrendous xenophobic attack on a hostel for refugees in the east German town of Hoyerswerda occurred. The attack resulted in the removal of the refugees from the hostel, as the perpetrators (neighbours and white German youths) had in fact intended. The perceived 'success' of this attack appeared to be a catalyst for further racist attacks, and the level of racially motivated crime has remained very high ever since. For example, in 1993, the Federal Criminal Police Office registered 6,721 xenophobic attacks and 3,840 attacks with an extreme right-wing motivation.[1] This represents an unprecedented level of racial violence for post-war Germany. Moreover, it is widely believed that the number of unreported cases is substantially higher, as many victims of racially motivated crime are reluctant to report such incidents to the statutory agencies.[2]

More recently, the phenomenon of racist violence within the German police force has caught the attention of the public nationally and internationally. In 1994 several cases of racist attacks allegedly committed by police officers were made public in Hamburg and Berlin. Following these reports the media and a number of criminologists claimed that severe xenophobic and racist tendencies were widely prevalent within the entire German police force.[3] This impression was reinforced by an Amnesty International report on police violence against foreigners and ethnic minorities in Germany which was published in May 1995. Amnesty's report accused the statutory agencies

---

1. *Verfassungsschutzbericht* 1993, p.79ff.

2. Comparable research for Britain shows that while 7,793 racial incidents were officially reported by the British Crime Survey, the real number of attacks was assumed to be as high as 140,000 incidents per year, *The Independent*, 15 July 1993.

3. The criminologist Monika Frommel states that the police not only show reluctance to combat racist incidents but actually engage in xenophobic activities. See 'Die Polizei, dein Feind und Schläger?' *Die Woche*, 22 September 1994.

of complacency and stated that there was a lack of commitment within the force to tackling the problem.[4]

## Legislative measures against racially motivated crime

The German legislative framework provides a number of measures which can be employed to counter the phenomenon of racially motivated crime. First, a comprehensive prohibition of discrimination on the basis of race is included in the Basic Law (*Grundgesetz*) of the Federal Republic of Germany. Article 1 of the Basic Law reads as follows:

1. The dignity of man shall be inviolable. To respect and protect it shall be the duty of all state authority.

2. The German people therefore acknowledge inviolable and inalienable human rights as the basis of every community, of peace and of justice in the world.

3. The following basic rights shall bind the legislature, the executive and the judiciary as directly enforceable law.

In addition to the right to human dignity, Article 3 para. 3 of the Basic Law guarantees the prohibition of racial discrimination:

No one may be disadvantaged or favoured because of his sex, his parentage, his race, his language, his homeland and origin, his faith, or his religion or political opinions.

Secondly, the German Criminal Code (*Strafgesetzbuch* (StGB)) contains special provisions designed to combat racially motivated crime. For example:

● Section 86 StGB makes the dissemination of propaganda materials of unconstitutional organisations subject to criminal liability.

● Section 86a StGB makes the use of emblems or symbols of certain parties and organisations, especially those of former National Socialist organisations, a criminal offence.

● Section 130 StGB makes it an offence to attack the human dignity of another in a manner likely to disturb the public peace, by inciting hatred against sections of the population, by fomenting arbitrary or violent acts against them, or by insulting, maliciously degrading or defaming them.

● Section 131 StGB provides that it is an offence to disseminate, publicly exhibit, post, demonstrate or otherwise make accessible, manufacture, procure, supply, store, offer, advertise, import or export literature, sound

---

4. Amnesty International, *Ausländer als Opfer: Polizeiliche Misshandlungen in der Bundesrepublik*, May 1995, AI-Index: EUR 23/06/95. In 1994 several police officers were charged with causing injury (*Körperverletzung im Amt*). However, preliminary proceedings (*Ermittlungsverfahren*) against police officers are very rarely brought to court (*Anklageerhebung*), and if charges are brought against an officer, the majority of cases end in an acquittal. For example in Berlin, 646 preliminary proceedings were started in 1992 against police officers with the suspicion of 'injury caused by a police officer'. Only 19 cases were brought to court and all of them led to an acquittal. See 'Schwarze Horden', *Der Spiegel*, 3 August 1994, p.109.

or picture recordings, illustrations or representations that incite racial hatred.

Sections 130 and 131 StGB are among the most important provisions of the German Criminal Code for combating right-wing extremist and xenophobic propaganda. In addition, the relevant sections of the Criminal Code are of course used to prosecute other offences where racial motivation is an aggravating factor.

The German government regards the provisions made through the legal instruments of the Basic Law and Criminal Code as sufficient for the appropriate prosecution and punishment of racially motivated crime. Following the drastic increase in xenophobic and right-wing extremist incidents, however, a number of specific problems of a legal and material nature became apparent, and the Suppression of Crime Act (*Verbrechensbekämpfungsgesetz*) was drawn up to address them. It came into force on 1 December 1994. The most important provisions are:

- The use of emblems or symbols that might be confused with those of unconstitutional organisations as listed under section 86a is a criminal offence. Previously it was unclear whether the use of variants of the emblems and symbols of banned National Socialist organisations (such as the swastika) was also unlawful.

- The production and stock-piling of propaganda material and emblems or symbols of unconstitutional organisations for the purpose of export, as well as their actual export, is a criminal offence.

- Anyone who, in a manner likely to disturb the public peace, condones, denies or plays down the genocide committed under National Socialist rule, or who disseminates or makes public writings with comparable content, is criminally liable. This provision is intended to ensure that such acts can be punished as criminal agitation to a greater extent than in the past.

- The range of punishment has been increased for offences involving bodily harm. Although this measure does not apply only to racially motivated incidents, the government sees this step as an affirmation of the importance it attaches to physical integrity.

- Expedited proceedings are now available for hearing cases with straightforward facts or clear evidence, so that punishment follows the crime as quickly as possible.

- Section 112a StGB was amended to allow a defendant to be remanded in custody in order to avert the danger of further offences, even if he or she had not, as was generally necessary in the past, been sentenced to imprisonment for a similar offence within the past five years. The revision is based on knowledge acquired primarily through combating racially motivated crime that certain offenders can only be prevented from committing further offences through remand in custody.

● The imposition of remand custody for certain grave offences has been extended to offences of 'specially aggravated arson' or 'wilfully causing grievous bodily harm'.

● Improvements have been introduced to the information system used by criminal prosecution authorities, and should benefit the handling of all cases, not just those involving racially motivated crimes.

As the Suppression of Crime Act has only been in force since December 1994, it remains to be seen whether the above amendments to the Criminal Code will have the desired effect.

Another important change was instituted by the amendment of the law concerning indemnification for victims of violent crimes (*Opfer-entschädigungsgesetz*). Before 1993 it was virtually impossible for non-German victims to receive any kind of indemnification, unless there were mutual arrangements between Germany and the country of origin. Under the impact of the horrendous wave of xenophobic and racist crime in Germany, the law was changed so that foreign victims in certain circumstances qualify for indemnification. The law was made retroactive to 1 July 1990 when a number of large scale racist attacks took place. However, foreign nationals who are in Germany for a short stay (less than three years) are eligible to only a restricted form of indemnification.[5]

### The political response

Apart from the legal measures against racism and xenophobia, German society as a whole was faced with a new political challenge. It was widely assumed that the large number of racially motivated incidents was also a consequence of the emotionally charged political debates on the new asylum law. The Federal Minister of Justice, Sabine Leutheusser-Schnarrenberger, described the new political climate in the following terms:

> ... in Germany the realisation is gradually gaining ground that, while the mostly young arsonists and perpetrators of violent crimes must in fact be prosecuted consistently under criminal law, the crimes committed by them are however only the visible expression of an on the whole much more dangerous extreme right mentality among parts of society that can no longer be ignored ...[6]

Awareness of this new political situation led to the realisation that xenophobia and right-wing extremism pose a serious challenge both to the state and society alike. A multitude of activities were initiated, ranging from anti-racist demonstrations and voluntary support groups to legislative changes and participation in activities of the European Union such as the European

---

5. 'Der Staat hilft den Opfern von Gewalttaten', *Bundesministerium für Arbeit*, Bonn, 1994.

6. *The Situation of Foreigners in Germany: Facts, Analyses, Arguments on Hostility towards Foreigners*, Press and Information Office of the Federal Government, Foreign Affairs Division, Bonn, January 1995, p.30.

Consultative Commission on Racism and Xenophobia, better known as the Kahn Committee.[7]

However, on a daily basis, most of the problems connected with racially motivated crime arise, and have to be dealt with, at local level. Consequently, responsibility for the protection of residents from ethnic minorities and the prevention of racially motivated crime lies largely with the individual *Länder* (states) and the cities themselves. In order to evaluate the effectiveness of the measures adopted to counter racially motivated crime, it is therefore necessary to look at the initiatives in a city with a substantial proportion of ethnic minorities.

This report examines the statutory responses to racially motivated crime in the city of Frankfurt am Main. Frankfurt was chosen because it has the largest ethnic minority population in Germany, a long history of immigration, and was the first city in Germany to establish a race relations unit as an integral part of the city council. The report looks at the political strategies employed by the various local agencies in the field of combating racially motivated crime and how these are put into practice in the daily routine of dealing with offenders and victims of racist incidents. In order to evaluate the position of Frankfurt regionally and nationally, the links between local policy actors and regional and national institutions are also mentioned when relevant.[8]

## FRANKFURT AS A MULTI-ETHNIC CITY

Frankfurt is the city with the highest percentage of foreign residents in Germany. According to the latest official statistics, 28.4 per cent (185,861) of the total population (654,388) are people from ethnic minorities holding foreign passports.[9] About 15 per cent of the non-German residents in Frankfurt were born in the city (mostly children of the former *Gastarbeiter* (guest workers), who have settled down in Germany). Of these, 23 per cent have lived in the city for more than 15 years, 29 per cent between five and 15 years, and only 32 per cent for less than five years. The percentage of non-German schoolchildren is even higher: 37 per cent of children and adolescents under the age of 18 are from immigrant families, and 78 per cent of all non-German pre-school children were born in Frankfurt.

---

7. 'Rassismus und Fremdenfeindlichkeit', *Tätigkeiten der Beratenden Kommission Rassismus und Fremdenfeindlichkeit*, Schlussbericht, Bruxelles, April 1995.

8. The report is based on a study conducted in Frankfurt in 1994/95. The research is based on information obtained from archives, case files, written information and interviews conducted with various representatives of statutory and non-governmental agencies.

9. *Statistische Porträts: Ausländer und Ausländerinnen in Frankfurt am Main*, Amt für Statistik, Wahlen und Einwohnerwesen, 29 August 1995. In comparison, the proportions of foreigners in some other big German cities are: Berlin 11.7 per cent, Stuttgart 22.7 per cent, Köln 18.7 per cent, München 21.9 per cent (Source: 'Grossstädte', *Statistisches Jarhbuch Deutscher Gemeinden*, 1994).

The percentage of foreign residents varies substantially in different parts of the city. Bahnhofsviertel, the area around Frankfurt am Main station, has the highest concentration, with 79 per cent of foreign residents. Other inner city areas have an average of around 55 per cent. The outer areas of Harheim, Nieder Erlenbach and Kalenbach, with around ten per cent, have the lowest percentage of foreign residents.[10]

Frankfurt, being an international centre of commerce and trade, is proud to call itself a city with a long and liberal tradition of immigration. People from different countries and cultures have always played an important role in the history of the city. For example, as early as the sixteenth century members of the Dutch Reformed Church fled to Frankfurt, where they set up new industries. In the seventeenth century, the French Huguenots who came to Frankfurt quickly established a strong position in the city's commercial life. They also had a lasting cultural influence – many surnames of French origin and Frankfurt idioms stem from that time.

It is important to note that Frankfurt's ethnic minority population is remarkably heterogeneous. First, Frankfurt's vicinity to the international airport makes the city an important transit zone. A multitude of people ranging from business people to asylum seekers enter the country through Frankfurt. As the main German centre for international business, Frankfurt is also home to a large number of companies, banks, press agencies and publishing firms from all over the world. For example, employees of large American, British, Japanese, French and Korean enterprises constitute about five per cent of the city's population. However, the largest minority group in Frankfurt still comprises guest workers and their families who arrived from the traditional recruitment countries from the 1950s and 1960s onwards.[11]

The long presence of people from different cultural and national backgrounds in Frankfurt explains why the city describes itself as multicultural and multi-ethnic. It is this image of the city that led to the establishment of the Department of Multicultural Affairs (DMA) as part of Frankfurt's city council. The DMA, which fulfils the function of a race relations unit, is still the only one of its kind in Germany. Furthermore, the city has established a separate Parliament for Foreigners (*Kommunale Ausländervertretung*) partly as compensation for their lack of voting rights.

## Racially motivated crime in Frankfurt

In Frankfurt, as in the rest of the country, the number of racially motivated attacks has risen since 1991. In 1993 146 racial attacks were registered by the police in the Frankfurt region. In the *Land* of Hesse 654 racial attacks were reported, the majority of them directed against Turkish people. Frankfurt has the largest number of attacks in absolute figures in the *Land* of Hesse.

---

10. *Statistisches Jahrbuch der Stadt Frankfurt*, 1993.

11. For example, 19 per cent of the ethnic minority population in Frankfurt comes from Turkey, 24.8 per cent from former Yugoslavia and 8.6 per cent from Italy. See *Statistische Porträts. Ausländer und Ausländerinnen in Frankfurt*, Amt für Statistik, Wahlen und Einwohnerwesen, 1995.

However, 60 per cent of all racially motivated attacks occur in small towns of up to 20,000 inhabitants.[12] Why is the level of racially motivated crime in Frankfurt apparently lower than in many other European cities of comparable size? Is the small number of officially registered attacks really evidence of the relative absence of racially motivated crime?

Most of the representatives of the city council, the police or the public prosecution service maintained that the long tradition of immigration to the city and its liberal political tradition, which has always favoured immigration for the benefit of trade and commerce, were probably responsible for the absence of xenophobic tendencies among large sections of the city's population. They also attributed the good relations between different ethnic groups in the city to the coalition between the Social Democratic Party (*Sozialdemokratische Partei Deutschland* (SPD)) and the Green Party (*Bündnis 90/Die Grünen*), as advocates of multicultural local politics. Finally, they referred to the speed with which the media and statutory agencies like the city council, the police and the public prosecution service issued public statements condemning any racially motivated attack in the city, thereby supposedly ensuring that xenophobic tendencies did not receive the tacit consent of statutory agencies that could be observed in some other German cities.

This view of Frankfurt as a racially harmonious city is not fully shared by many members of non-governmental organisations nor by a few representatives of the DMA. They doubt that many victims of xenophobic attacks approach the statutory agencies either to report a case or to ask for help and advice. They also believe that the official registration procedures are unsystematic and that the political will to register an incident as racially motivated is lacking, especially in the case of the police.

It is difficult to estimate the number of racially motivated attacks which do not come to the attention of the statutory agencies. However, it is possible to say whether the official registration procedures are appropriate to pick up all cases with a potential racial motivation. It is also possible to look at some aspects of the prevention of racially motivated crime and at the extent to which anti-racist policies are put into practice in the daily routines of the various statutory agencies. We can ask, for example, whether they cooperate in the field and try to complement each other's work, and how they respond to victims of xenophobic attacks.

## STATUTORY RESPONSES TO RACIALLY MOTIVATED CRIME IN FRANKFURT

The efforts of statutory agencies in combating racially motivated crime fall into two main areas: prevention and repression. The following section examines these areas of work and how they are undertaken by the different policy actors in the field.

---

12. *Landeslagebild Fremdenfeindliche Straftaten in Hessen 1 Jan-31 Dec*, Hessisches Landeskriminalamt 1993, Wiesbaden 1994.

## The police

The police in Frankfurt are subject to directives from the *Land* Criminal Police Office of Hesse (*Hessisches Landeskriminalamt*). At the end of 1991 a comprehensive strategy to tackle racially motivated crime was drawn up by the Criminal Police Office and, with a few local additions and alterations, was immediately implemented in Frankfurt.

### Prevention of racially motivated crime

A public relations scheme was devised to increase public awareness of racially motivated crime. The scheme laid special emphasis on the ethnic minority population in order to increase their trust in the police and to encourage them to report racially motivated incidents. In Frankfurt, the police held public meetings to introduce specially appointed community officers who were responsible for areas with large ethnic minority populations and for refugee hostels. Their task was to increase cooperation with the police and to advise people from ethnic minorities and refugees on ways of preventing arson and racist attacks. Citizens are constantly encouraged to inform the police if skinheads or right-wing youths cause any problems. To emphasise their political commitment to the safety of the ethnic minority population, the number of police officers patrolling the streets has been dramatically increased. The police in Frankfurt recently became the first force in Germany to produce a video film called *Notruf 110* (emergency call 110). The aim of the film is to encourage citizens to inform the police if they notice anything suspicious or have any knowledge about a crime, and to reduce the inhibitions that people from ethnic minorities appear to have about contacting the police. The film is available free of charge and in six different languages. It is widely seen throughout Germany as an example of good practice in police-community relations, and other cities intend to use the film as well.[13] Unfortunately, the film does not contain a specific section on racially motivated crime. The message of the film is reinforced by leaflets written in the relevant minority languages which the police, in cooperation with the city council and the fire brigade, have issued to ethnic minority households and minority organisations in the city.

Another important aspect of the efforts to prevent racially motivated incidents is the work done within the police force itself. In the past there have been allegations of insensitivity in police communications with ethnic minorities, and officers themselves acknowledged a lack of understanding about the different cultural codes and backgrounds in minority communities. In response to these concerns, the Frankfurt police introduced a variety of measures. First, special Commissioners for Foreigners (*Ausländerbeauftragte*) were introduced,[14] and in November 1993 two Turks and two Moroccans

---

13. 'Video-Clip als Hilfe: Notruf für Ausländer', *Frankfurter Rundschau*, 20 July 1993.

14. Most of the information about the Commissioners for Foreigners was obtained in interviews with the two commissioners, Nesrin Tavasolli-Aghdam and Nassif Khalil.

were appointed in the Criminal Investigation Department (CID) and the police force.[15] They are not part of the usual police force or CID and do not have any coercive powers (*hoheitliche Befugnisse*).[16] Their responsibilities are two-fold. On the one hand, they work as ethnic minority community officers, particularly with young people, and try to improve their relations with the police. The commissioners explain to young delinquents and their parents how the law works, because it is in this area that misunderstandings, and consequent suspicion of the police, are likely to arise. The commissioners also try to identify problem areas between white and ethnic minority youths that could lead to violent clashes.

On the other hand, the Commissioners for Foreigners are responsible for instructing police officers on the cultural backgrounds of Frankfurt's ethnic minorities. They have drawn up guidelines on how to prevent misunderstandings, for example when making arrests or conducting body searches; they have conducted seminars at the police academy in Hessen and other training institutions, where the topics of racism, xenophobia and right-wing extremism have been introduced as an integral part of the curriculum; and, in cooperation with the city council's DMA, they have held additional seminars and workshops in Frankfurt to give police officers the opportunity to learn something about the cultural, social and political traditions of the different ethnic minority communities in the city.

A second initiative by the Frankfurt police, only indirectly connected with the prevention of racially motivated crime, was the recruitment of ethnic minority police officers. Apart from the obvious advantages of having officers who are fluent in the different local languages, the police regarded this as a positive and public sign of their commitment to minority communities. In general, foreigners are not permitted to join the civil service, but some *Länder* have decided to make an exception for the police force, and the *Land* of Hesse has recently started recruiting ethnic minority police officers. Police opinions about the initiative differed widely: some welcomed the measure, others were hostile. The number of new ethnic minority officers is still very small – between ten and 15 only are currently undergoing training, and it is too early to say whether the initiative has had any significant effects.

*Tackling racially motivated crime*

The Frankfurt police, in cooperation with the *Land* Criminal Police Office of Hesse, has initiated a range of measures to tackle racially motivated crime. The first step was to adopt a standard definition of a 'xenophobic offence', to avoid inconsistent practices in different police stations. The following definition is used throughout Germany:

---

15. Among Frankfurt's ethnic minorities, the Turkish and Moroccan communities have the highest delinquency rate.

16. The Commissioners for Foreigners were excluded from section 163 of the Code of Criminal Procedure (*Strafprozessordnung* (StPO)), which means that they are excluded from the normal officer's duty/right to investigate a case or take part in a criminal prosecution. See Polizei Frankfurt, *Die Ausländerbeauftragten der Frankfurter Polizei*, p.3.

Xenophobic criminal offences are offences directed against:

- persons, who, according to the intolerant view of the offender, have no right to temporary or permanent residence in Germany on the grounds of nationality, ethnic origin, race, colour, religion, philosophy of life, background or because of their appearance.

- persons/institutions/objects, where the offender acts for xenophobic motives.[17]

To make it easier for the individual officer to recognise right-wing extremist offences, the *Land* Criminal Police Office distributed information on different right-wing extremist organisations and their symbols and emblems to all police stations in the region. It also advised officers on the appropriate legal action for various criminal offences. According to the Director of the *Land* Criminal Police Office of Hesse, the sensitivity of police officers to this area has improved significantly as a result of the seminars and workshops on racially motivated crime, while the public commitment to combating racially motivated crime has led to greater willingness among the local population to report racially motivated incidents to the statutory agencies.

How do xenophobic or racist incidents come to the notice of the police in Frankfurt? They can be reported either by the victim or by the police themselves. For example, in cases of arson attacks on refugee hostels the police are obliged to investigate, even if no victim comes forward to report the incident. The majority of attacks are reported at local police stations. Fewer people inform the CID or the prosecuting authorities directly. According to one CID officer, people who approached the CID or the prosecuting authorities directly gave 'lack of trust in the local police officers' as a reason for not contacting the local police station.

The police in Frankfurt have no special racist incident form, which means that the registration of an incident as 'racially motivated' depends largely on the officer making the report. He or she has to decide whether the category of 'xenophobic criminal offence' applies to the case. If a racial motivation is suspected or reported by the victim or officer, this fact will be entered on the report, but there is no separate section on the registration form for racist incidents.

Racially motivated crime is dealt with in the CID, where two branches fairly high up in the hierarchy focus on xenophobia and right-wing extremism. They keep a central register where all racially motivated incidents reported to the police or prosecuting authorities are analysed and categorised. Any incident suspected to be, or identified as having, xenophobic and/or right-wing extremist motivations is automatically referred to this central register. According to the guidelines from the *Land* Criminal Police Office of Hesse, the CID sets up special investigation squads whenever necessary to work on urgent cases of xenophobic crime. For example, in July 1994 when two unidentified skinheads attacked and injured a man from Sierra Leone in central Frankfurt, a special unit was immediately set up, with officers brought in from other departments – there is no permanent investigation

---

17. See letter by the director, Mr Timm, *Hessisches Landeskriminalamt,* 27 June 1995.

squad with adequate staffing in the two relevant branches of the Frankfurt CID. Until the two suspects were found and questioned two weeks later, the special investigation squad worked exclusively on this case.[18]

The *Land* Criminal Police Office gives advice on mobilising public support through appeals for help and may offer financial rewards for information leading to the apprehension of racist perpetrators. Regular police meetings are held, both at local level and with the *Land* Criminal Police Office, to identify problem areas and focal points for xenophobic incidents and to make police operations more responsive to actual local need.

The Commissioners for Foreigners are also involved in tackling racially motivated crime. They act as contact points for racially motivated incidents, and provide an opportunity for victims to talk to them about their case. The commissioners also hold meetings at community centres and religious institutions in order to publicise their services to the ethnic minority population. One Commissioner for Foreigners said that she had established herself as a mediator in disputes that appear to be racially motivated. For example, on one occasion she tried to mediate in a dispute between a Turkish man and a police officer on the street. The officer wanted to charge the Turkish man for insulting him – the Turkish man thought that the officer had racially abused him. The commissioner attempted to reach a settlement out of court and, although she was not successful in this case, she believes that the concept of mediation will work in the long run. Another Commissioner for Foreigners mentioned plans to establish an obligatory routine procedure whereby commissioners would be informed of all cases of alleged racism before a formal complaint was lodged. This would simplify their work: they could speak to the victims in their mother tongue – victims, it was believed, put greater trust in the commissioners than in other police officers; and the process for handling racially motivated crime would be more consistent and controllable. These plans have already been discussed and approved in principle by the management of the CID. However, no steps have been taken so far to put them into practice.

The main weakness of the role of the Commissioners for Foreigners, both in preventing and tackling racially motivated crime, is that it is merely advisory. None of their recommendations are compulsory for police officers. One commissioner said that the commissioners needed greater autonomy. The hierarchical structure of the police force, she said, made their work more difficult, although, on the positive side, their 'lack of power' probably made it easier for the police to accept them – as advisers, the commissioners were not perceived as a threat. Overall, after 15 months in the job, the Commissioners for Foreigners feel well accepted both in the police force and the CID.

*Racism in the police force*

The phenomenon of racist incidents within the police force has received considerable public attention throughout Germany. Amnesty International's

---

18. See case study 1, p.52.

report on police racism found that in Germany '... a clear pattern of maltreatment of foreigners and ethnic minorities by the police is visible'. The report focused on the police force in Berlin, as half the cases reported to Amnesty took place in the German capital.

Judging by the number of cases officially reported to the statutory agencies, the problem did not appear to be as extensive in Frankfurt as in Berlin: the Amnesty report included only one case of a racist attack by Frankfurt police officers. At management level, the Frankfurt police are clearly aware that there are xenophobic tendencies among some sections of the force. For example, in a widely publicised document, the Police Commissioner (Polizeipräsident) asked all officers to distance themselves from right-wing political movements.[19] Despite this political commitment, frequent reports on the maltreatment of ethnic minorities and refugees have been made to several non-governmental organisations and to the DMA. It is difficult to assess the veracity of these allegations, as very often no concrete details of incidents are mentioned. We were told quite often during interviews that victims were very reluctant to report racial attacks committed by police officers to the statutory agencies, either because they feared further victimisation by the police or because they mistrusted the willingness of the police to investigate cases of alleged racism within their own ranks. One Commissioner for Foreigners in the CID said that, in her view, the ethnic minority population in Frankfurt were not well informed, either about their rights as citizens or about the powers of the police:

> Quite often there is the feeling among ethnic minorities that police officers have overstepped their legal rights, when in fact they have not. However, very often they do not complain, when it would be appropriate to do so.

Before evaluating police willingness to investigate allegations of racism within the force, it is important to look at the formal procedures for such investigations. Preliminary proceedings are initiated as soon as a racist attack is reported to the police by the victim or by a third person on behalf of the victim or by another police officer in Frankfurt, and the case is referred immediately to the public prosecution service for independent investigation. The press officer for the police said when interviewed that an officer suspected of a racially motivated offence, was, as a rule, temporarily suspended from duty until the investigation was closed. However, there has been at least one case where none of the accused officers was suspended from duty at any stage of the investigation.[20] Irrespective of the outcome of the public prosecution service's investigation, disciplinary proceedings always follow when criminal proceedings result in a conviction. If the officer is sentenced to at least one year in prison, he or she is immediately dismissed. Shorter sentences usually lead to an admonishment or fine or demotion, although, depending on the severity and nature of the offence, they can also result in dismissal.

---

19. See Franzke, Bettina, *Die Polizei in Kontakt und Konflikt mit Menschen ausländischer Herkunft*, Frankfurt 1993, p.4.

20. See case study 3, p.56.

In Frankfurt, there were a number of investigations of allegations of maltreatment of ethnic minorities in police custody. The interviewed police officers and the Commissioners for Foreigners maintained that the investigations were carried out correctly and that there were no structural defects in the formal investigative procedures. Furthermore, it was claimed that allegations of racism were often made by ethnic minority delinquents who wanted to discredit certain officers. Another officer stated that many of the cases of alleged maltreatment in police custody were in reality '… appropriate responses to the violent behaviour of ethnic minority suspects'.

However, a closer look at the formal procedures does reveal some structural weaknesses, notwithstanding the political commitment to combat racism within the force. First, the fact that officers accused of racist offences are usually interrogated by other police officers, who might even be their colleagues, is problematic. It is common practice for the police to conduct the first interrogations on behalf of the public prosecution service,[21] and it is vital that in such cases the public prosecution service should immediately take on the entire investigation to avoid the danger of any attempt to cover up the incident. Secondly, it is often the case that accusations of racist assault are countered by the charge of obstructing an officer in the performance of his duties (*Widerstand gegen die Staatsgewalt*). If this charge is brought against a victim, the accused officer can easily explain the injuries sustained as the result of having to use proportionate force (*verhältnismässige Gewaltanwendung*). Charges of obstruction are probably not brought by police officers initially, in order to avoid too many judicial proceedings of a trivial nature. However, they are frequently brought when officers are suspected of racially motivated maltreatment, and it is difficult to avoid the impression that they are merely attempts to deflect attention from the original offence. Two cases of alleged police racism were examined for this study. While the formal procedure appears to have worked satisfactorily in one case, serious questions have been raised about the police and public prosecution service's investigation in the other.[22]

### The public prosecution service

Responsibility for handling cases of racially motivated crime lies with the Political Department (*Politische Abteilung*) of the public prosecution service. The department has four public prosecutors, one of whom is solely responsible for xenophobic and right-wing extremist crime. This post has been in existence for at least three years (the public prosecutor responsible for this area in Frankfurt could not say when exactly the post had been established). In addition, one public prosecutor is responsible for allegations of racially motivated crime by police officers on duty.

By definition, the public prosecution service is not involved in the prevention of crime; its work lies in the area of tackling crime. The public

---

21. See section 161 StPO.

22. See case study 3, pp.56-7.

prosecutor can be informed about a suspected racially motivated crime by the police, by the victim, or by anyone who happens to know about the incident (*Strafanzeige*). If the suspicion is confirmed from the public prosecutor's point of view, he or she can then institute legal proceedings (*Strafantrag stellen*).

When racially motivated crime was on the increase all over Germany, the Ministry of Justice in Hesse called monthly meetings in order to assess the situation in different cities, and to ensure that public prosecutors in Hesse were being consistent in their evaluation of cases with a xenophobic or right-wing extremist motivation. A number of seminars and conferences were held for judges, public prosecutors, probation and youth officers and victim support agencies. These conferences led to the realisation that only strong inter-agency cooperation would lead to an appropriate strategy against racially motivated crime.[23]

The public prosecutor has to follow definitions and guidelines drawn up by the Federal Ministry of Justice and the Ministry of Justice in Hesse. Two racist incident forms are routinely filled in, and information passed on monthly to the Ministry of Justice in Hesse where regional statistics are compiled. Information is produced on the number of xenophobic and right-wing extremist attacks,[24] and on various characteristics of the crime including:

- Nationality of the victim

- Facts of the case

- Factors suggesting an organised crime (xenophobic or right-wing extremist groups)

- Information about a potential financial reward (*Auslobung*)

- Procedural facts such as
  - date of registration of the case by the police
  - when the case was referred to the public prosecution
  - when the suspects were identified
  - whether a warrant for the suspects' arrest was issued
  - when the case was brought to court, or abandoned
  - when the verdict was pronounced
  - whether the suspects were sentenced or acquitted.

The racist incident forms are quite useful for assessing the action taken by the public prosecution service. The list below shows how often the different sections of the Criminal Code relevant to prosecution of racially motivated crime (which are printed on the forms) were used. In Frankfurt, the number of criminal proceedings instituted in 1994 were as follows:

---

23. See *Bericht über die Umsetzung der politischen Initiativen der Hessischen Landesregierung zur Eindämmung des Rechtsextremismus und seiner Ursachen*, Hessische Landesregierung,1994, pp.8-11.

24. See Appendix 1, p.63 for the number of attacks recorded by the public prosecution service in 1994.

| | |
|---|---|
| Sections 86, 86a: | 135 |
| Sections 125, 125a: | 2 |
| Sections 130, 131 | 29 |
| Section 185f | 12 |
| Section 211, 212 | 1 |
| Section 223f | 6 |
| Section 126, 241 etc | 15 |
| Section 303f | 3 |
| Section 340 | 1 |

The forms also indicate whether cases of racially motivated crime are processed without delay. In the past, there had been complaints that some German courts and public prosecutors tended to sit on such cases. In response, and to control the public prosecutors, the forms were amended to provide information about the duration of the investigation and the court case. The public prosecutor is also required to report to the Ministry of Justice in Hesse during the case. However, in at least one case there seems to have been a substantial delay on the part of the public prosecutor in processing a case of alleged police racism.[25]

When interviewed, the public prosecutor said that racial incidents were handled with special care in Frankfurt. He claimed that cases which would usually be dismissed because of the trifling nature of the offence (*wegen Geringfügigkeit eingestellt*) were never abandoned if there was any suspicion of a xenophobic motivation, and that even if the suspicion proved false, the public prosecutor's office did not give this too much publicity.[26] Further evidence of the strong commitment of the public prosecution service in Frankfurt to combating racially motivated crime came from its response in the case of grievous bodily harm where skinheads beat up a man from Sierra Leone (see p. 55): the public prosecution service, in cooperation with the city council, made public statements and offered a large financial reward – an amount usually reserved for cases of murder – for information leading to the apprehension of the suspects.[27] The public prosecutor also maintained that the sentences for racially motivated crimes were generally higher than those in comparable cases without this factor, but he was unable to prove this assertion.

Finally, the public prosecution service, in cooperation with the police, has instituted certain standard procedures to simplify the processing of cases. For example, in the case of a well-known Jewish MP who regularly received a large number of racist letters, a procedure was agreed by the victim, the

---

25. See case study 3, p.56-7.

26. Compare case study 5, p.59.

27. See case study 2, p.55.

police and the public prosecutor, as it would have been very complicated and time-consuming to report each case individually.[28] The procedure reduced the amount of work for the victim and also significantly reduced the number of cases for the public prosecution service. Judging by this example, inter-agency cooperation with the police is working well, with responses to racially motivated crime being organised according to need.

## Frankfurt City Council and Local Authority

The highest political decision-making body in Frankfurt is the city council (*Stadtverordnetenversammlung*). The councillors (*Stadtverordnete*) are directly elected in local elections for a period of four years. As well as the councillors, the citizens of Frankfurt elect representatives (*Ortsbeiräte*) for advisory bodies in each ward. These advisory bodies were established to guarantee a close connection between the town hall and the needs of the citizens. The city's administration is headed by the municipal authority (*Magistrat*). The heads of the local authority departments are elected by the council, whereas the mayor is directly elected by Frankfurt's citizens.[29]

Since the 1989 elections the council has been run by an SPD-Green Party coalition, but the mayor belongs to the Christian Democratic Party (*Christlich Demokratische Union* (CDU)). The fascist *Nationaldemokratische Partei Deutschlands* (NPD) gained a surprising amount of support. This was partly because the CDU's strategy of trying to win votes through anti-semitic and racist canvassing was a complete failure. Instead of voting for the CDU, 20 per cent of the electorate turned to the right-wing extremist NPD. Once in office, the SPD-Green coalition decided to establish a Department for Multicultural Affairs in the city council in order to counter the manifest racist tendencies among a large section of Frankfurt's population. However, the Department did not receive unanimous support from the SPD – not all party members wanted to acknowledge that Germany was a country of immigration and that discrimination and racism were powerful forces in Frankfurt. Finally, the newly-elected mayor, Volker Hauff, appointed Daniel Cohn-Bendit as political spokesperson for multicultural affairs with a seat on the city council. The spokesperson has the right to address the assemblies and to take part in the decision-making processes of the city council. At the same time, the Department for Multicultural Affairs (*Amt für Multikulturelle Angelegenheiten*) was established as part of the city's administrative structure.

### Department for Multicultural Affairs (DMA)

Daniel Cohn-Bendit has political responsibility for the DMA's work in the city council. He works on an honorary basis. Internally, the department is led by the chief executive, Rosi Wolf-Almanasreh, and has 16 members of staff, each with specific areas of responsibility. The staff are evenly divided

---

28. See case study 1, p.54.

29. See *Handbuch der Stadtverordnetenversammlung*, Stadt Frankfurt am Main, XIII, Wahlperiode, pp.7-8.

between German and non-German, and male and female employees. The department's remit was initially defined in the following administrative decree by the mayor in 1989:

- Mediation in cases of conflict between different cultures and between council departments and those cultures. To work out strategies to solve those conflicts.

- Development of ideas in city planning in order to establish a multi-cultural urbanism.

- Dealing with the problems of ethnic minority youths.

- Furthering of migrants' cultures and cultural initiatives, which serve the purpose of inter-cultural harmony.

- Exchange programmes for youth organisations in cooperation with schools, organisations and youth centres.

- Looking after refugees.

- Working as a Commissioner for Foreigners' Affairs.[30]

Although the decree gives the DMA a certain amount of authority, the chief executive does not feel adequately empowered to influence the city's anti-racist policies effectively. She is currently campaigning for a council policy that makes it compulsory for all other council departments to cooperate with the DMA, and to pass on information.

Generally speaking, the DMA is well accepted both at local level by the local authority and the city's population, and nationally. For example, in 1990 the city of Frankfurt received a special award from a human rights organisation for setting up the DMA,[31] and the concept of an internal Department for Foreigners' Affairs within the local administration is referred to throughout Germany as the 'Frankfurt model'. However, the work of the DMA has also resulted in constant animosity towards its representatives. Daniel Cohn-Bendit and Rosi Wolf-Almanasreh, the chief executive, are frequent targets of racist threats and racist mail, ranging from anti-semitic propaganda to murder threats. According to a DMA report on this subject, the public prosecution service has been very reluctant to follow up complaints from the DMA, and has so far been unable to trace the perpetrators.[32] By contrast, the police are mentioned as being very committed to investigating racist threats to the DMA.[33]

As a result of their own experience of xenophobic and racist attacks, and the sometimes ambivalent attitude of the judicial agencies towards this problem, the issue of racially motivated crime occupies a central position in the work of the DMA. The chief executive identified two main areas of work in this field: public relations activity and individual case work. The department's

---

30. See Leggewie, Claus, *MultiKulti. Spielregeln für die Vielvölkerrepublik*, Nördlingen 1990, p.46.

31. See *Zweieinhalb Jahre Amt für Multikulturelle Angelegenheiten, zusammengestellt von Rosi Wolf-Almanasreh*, Amt für Multikulturelle Angelegenheiten, Frankfurt 1993, p.21.

32. *Ibid.* p.26.

33. *Ibid.*

public relations efforts were directed at raising public consciousness about racism and discrimination through events and posters in council departments. They included:

- Submission of proposals to the city council to include anti-discrimination rules in the town charter and in the terms of contracts for council civil servants and employees. (The city council did not accept the proposal, because civil servants are already prohibited from discriminating against anyone under section 7 of the civil service law (*Beamtenrechtsrahmengesetz*) and a separate statement, in its view, would be superfluous.)

- Statements and proposals to national and *Länder* authorities in the field of racism and anti-discrimination (for example, participation in the National Working Committee on the Possibility of Anti-Discrimination Legislation for Germany).

- Lectures at police stations on intercultural conflicts and different cultural traditions. (After an initial trial period, these lectures are now a regular feature of DMA-police cooperation.)

- Meetings with relevant agencies to establish regular cooperation.

The DMA's main activity is individual casework. As it has no judicial power, it works very much as a mediating agency, arranging meetings between the parties involved in cases of insults, neighbour disputes, and so on. Any alleged offender who refuses to participate in the DMA's mediation efforts is threatened with legal proceedings. The DMA also tries to mediate in conflicts between council officers and ethnic minority citizens. If a client of the council or a citizen accuses a council officer of racist or discriminatory behaviour, the DMA has the power to initiate disciplinary measures against employees of other departments if the allegation is confirmed and initial mediation efforts have failed.

Ninety per cent of all requests to the DMA for help are made by ethnic minority residents.[34] According to the chief executive, in the majority of cases the intervention by the DMA is successful. If all efforts at reaching a settlement out of court fail, the department supports victims of racial attacks during the necessary legal proceedings. In this area of work, the DMA has established firm and regular links with the Commissioners for Foreigners in the Frankfurt police force and refers victims to them.

The bulk of the cases reported directly to the DMA concern neighbour disputes and racist attacks, most of which are allegedly committed by police officers. The DMA does not have the power to provide legal counselling, but its staff often write to the relevant police department to follow up complaints and to negotiate on behalf of the victims. They also refer the victims to lawyers specialising in the field of anti-racism, and try to mobilise other agencies. The DMA does not have a formal system for recording such cases, and when a complaint is lodged, it depends largely on the employee

---

34. *Ibid.* p.58.

handling the case whether the information is entered in the appropriate file. Despite this somewhat haphazard way of recording incidents, the DMA has a substantial collection of cases involving racial motivation.

In addition to the work described above, the DMA seeks to cooperate with other local authority departments. While it has supervisory responsibilities, and the right therefore to investigate other departments if there is any suspicion of racially motivated misconduct or malpractice, the DMA also tries to establish good working relations with other departments and to ensure that their administrative functions are carried out without any discrimination. A number of DMA employees work mainly in this area, and serve other departments as consultants on multi-ethnic issues. The importance placed on cooperation is further reflected in the numerous interdepartmental working groups meeting on a regular basis.[35] The chief executive maintained that it was because of this emphasis on cooperation rather than control that the DMA's supervisory role was accepted by the other council departments. The frequency of requests for help with multi-ethnic issues from other departments also suggests that the DMA has established itself as an integral part of the administration, and that it uses its position to create a comprehensive local authority strategy for racial equality.

The supervisory role of the DMA is also seen as a signal to the ethnic minority population that redress against discrimination can be found within the administrative structure itself. For example, in September 1994 a multi-agency group was formed to resolve an inter-ethnic conflict between a number of Romany and German families. The Department of Social Services (*Sozialamt*), which was approached by the political advisory body (*Ortsbeirat*) of the ward where the conflict arose, set up a working group with representatives from the DMA and a Romany organisation to assess the situation. Several meetings were held with residents of the area and the conflict was defused.[36]

### The Youth Welfare Department (Jugendamt)

Like the DMA, the Youth Welfare Department (YWD) is very active in combating racially motivated crime. In the area of crime prevention, the YWD sees its main task as that of overcoming xenophobia and racist misconceptions among young people in Frankfurt and has initiated a wide range of measures. For example, the YWD regularly holds multicultural events and has set up several multi-ethnic youth centres. One member of the department said that the lack of ethnic minority employees was a real problem for the YWD at a day to day level, as the majority of its clients were from ethnic minorities; while a social worker thought that the presence of ethnic minority social workers would help to emphasise to white young Germans the fact that they live in a multi-ethnic society. However, not many ethnic minority candidates qualfed for social work and even fewer applied for jobs as social

---

35. *Ibid.* pp.39-41.

36. 'Sozialarbeiter sollen vermitteln. Stadt will Konflikt um acht Roma-Familien entschärfen', *Frankfurter Allgemeine Zeitung*, 13 September 1994.

workers with the YWD. On the other hand, a number of ethnic minority organisations claimed that the YWD was unwilling to employ ethnic minority social workers and that there were plenty of ethnic minority candidates for jobs with the YWD, but that they had been rejected. For example, one ethnic minority youth worker claimed that while 80-90 per cent of the young people visiting municipal youth centres belong to ethnic minorities, only one to two per cent of the employees come from the minority population. It was impossible to verify these claims during the research.

Another YWD initiative in the area of crime prevention is the introduction of so-called 'street workers' who meet young people at youth centres and elsewhere in order to detect potential conflict and to defuse potentially dangerous situations. The initiative appears to be effective, as the number of inter-ethnic conflicts is apparently very low in Frankfurt.

The YWD's main role is to tackle racially motivated crime through the help it was legally set up to provide to juvenile and adolescent offenders between 14 and 20 years of age. This statutory service is also available for juvenile and adolescent offenders who have committed xenophobic or racist attacks. The social workers in the YWD, known as *Jugendgerichtshilfe*, work closely with the offenders at all stages of the legal proceedings, and try to establish their personal backgrounds and motivations. In cases of racially motivated crime, social workers are required to write a report for the court assessing the offender's attitudes towards ethnic minorities. For example, in the case of the two skinheads who beat up a man from Sierra Leone, the social worker proposed anti-violence training for one of the perpetrators,[37] as she thought that this would be more effective than a prison sentence in changing his views about ethnic minorities. In some cases, the reports for the court do not put enough emphasis on the offender's racist or xenophobic motivations. The social workers are expected to continue their work with the perpetrators after the trial, or imprisonment, to help them to break away from their old patterns of xenophobic behaviour. However, due to a shortage of staff, this does not always happen.

A number of social workers said that they were frequently approached by ethnic minority young people complaining of racist behaviour by police or council officers. In such cases they would try to assist the young people if they decided to make a formal complaint, but none of the complaints appears so far to have led to the apprehension or punishment of the alleged perpetrator. Many social workers maintained that ethnic minority young people were more likely to be stopped and searched by the police on the streets and therefore constantly felt threatened and unfairly treated.

## POLITICAL REPRESENTATION OF ETHNIC MINORITIES

The most extraordinary feature of Frankfurt's political landscape is the existence of a local parliament for foreigners (*Kommunale Ausländervertretung* (KAV)). In Germany, ethnic minority residents with foreign passports have

---

37. See case study 2, p. 55.

no voting rights. Most German cities with a substantial ethnic minority population have consultation bodies or *Ausländerbeiräte*, but these are usually not representative of the minority population, and are marginalised in the political decision-making process. In Frankfurt, ethnic minority organisations increasingly began demanding more effective consultation, and the city council decided in 1991 to create a consultative forum which was more representative of the ethnic minority population and was able to take part in city politics. Elections for the KAV were held in December 1991. With the creation of this body, Frankfurt became the first German city to have directly elected representation for immigrants. Furthermore, the new bylaws (*Gemeindeordnung*) for the *Land* of Hesse, which came into force in 1993, included the KAV as an integral part of the political organisation of the city of Frankfurt. Still, the decisions of the KAV are not obligatory for the council, and the organisation only acts as a consulting agency for the ethnic minority population. The KAV is composed of 51 non-German representatives who are elected by Frankfurt's registered foreign residents. The chief executive is Bahman Nirumand, a well known writer and journalist of Iranian origin. The KAV is closely linked to the DMA and is even located in the same office. Legislative measures by the city council and local authority decisions are discussed by the KAV, and members have a right to take part in council and local authority meetings, to suggest changes and to comment publicly on ethnic minority politics. For example, in 1993, the city council accepted 31 per cent and rejected only nine per cent of the KAV's proposals.[38] Furthermore, the KAV sends representatives to all meetings of the consultative bodies at ward level and to all working committees of the council. However, it bears repeating that the organisation has no executive power – the chairman of the KAV has publicly complained that the city council views the organisation merely as a token of its tolerance and does not ascribe enough importance to it. According to the chairman, even the DMA is very hesitant to consult the KAV on all issues relevant to ethnic minorities.[39]

In the field of combating racially motivated crime, the KAV's main role is in the area of crime prevention. In 1993, the KAV had several meetings with the police and the city council to discuss the incidence of racially motivated crime in Frankfurt. The organisation has participated in several crime prevention schemes, such as the police video film, *Notruf 110* (see p. 36). The KAV chairman frequently addresses the city council emphasising the need for stronger commitment to anti-racist policies in the council's work.[40]

The KAV has issued a number of press releases condemning particular racially motivated attacks and urging the statutory agencies to respond with due force. For example, in the case of the skinhead attack on the man from Sierra Leone, the KAV appealed to the public to show solidarity with victims if they happened to witness a racially motivated attack.[41]

---

38. *Jahresbericht 1993, Stadtverordnetenversammlung,* Stadt Frankfurt am Main, 13 Wahlperiode, p.44.

39. *Ibid.* p.31.

40. *Kommunale Ausländer- und Ausländerinnenvertretung KAV, Jahresbericht 1993,* I. Wahlperiode, Frankfurt 1993, pp.40-44.

41. *Ibid.* p.75.

Recently, the KAV initiated the establishment of the new Commission for Equality and Integration, which is affiliated to the city council. This body is composed of councillors, citizens, local authority officers, trade unionists and KAV members. The aim of the Commission for Equality and Integration is to discuss the situation and problems of ethnic minority residents in Frankfurt. Issues connected with the prevention and repression of racially motivated crime are also expected to be part of the Commission's political agenda.

## NON-GOVERNMENTAL ORGANISATIONS AND VICTIM SUPPORT AGENCIES

In addition to the statutory agencies, there are a number of non-governmental organisations active in combating racially motivated crime. In the area of victim support, in particular, there is very little statutory provision and ethnic minority groups, non-governmental organisations and religious institutions try to fill this gap. The following are just a few examples of how some of these organisations are attempting to alleviate the effects of racially motivated crime on victims.

### SOS Rassismus

This citizens' initiative is comparable, and closely related, to the French initiative SOS Racisme.[42] The organisation campaigns publicly against xenophobic and racist tendencies in Frankfurt and sees itself as a contact point for victims of racism. The group accompanies victims to see lawyers, advises them on legal problems and provides some psychological counselling. For example, in the case of the victim from Sierra Leone,[43] the organisation helped the man with legal advice, paid for his lawyer, and accompanied him to all the court and legal hearings. In this case they also worked with the DMA, which was trying to support the victim.

A spokesperson for the organisation claimed that in Frankfurt the public prosecution service tends to delay cases of xenophobic attacks. SOS Rassismus therefore campaigns to press the statutory agencies for speedier processing of such cases. Finally, the organisation is part of a national network seeking to raise public consciousness of racism and xenophobia. The spokesperson maintained that creating networks, even at European level, is essential to maximise the success of such initiatives.

### Einwanderertreff

This is an ethnic minority organisation which was set up in 1990. Its aim is to be a contact point for Frankfurt's ethnic minority population on all questions concerning immigration, racially motivated crime, housing, and so on.

---

42. See Colette Smith's study of the situation in Lyons, pp. 67-98

43. See case study 2, p.55.

Its office serves as a meeting place for ethnic minorities and white Germans alike. All the staff are from ethnic minorities, which the chairman maintained was the reason that more cases of racist attacks came to their attention; he said that victims felt less reluctant to approach them than the statutory agencies. Besides the casework, Einwanderertreff is very active in the youth sector, work which it considers to be of great importance in the prevention of racially motivated crime.

Einwanderertreff does not have good relations with the statutory agencies in general, and the DMA in particular, as it blames the DMA for marginalising minority groups.

## Der Weisse Ring

This organisation is the only national victim support agency in Germany, and has a small branch in Frankfurt. Der Weisse Ring provides financial, legal, psychological and emotional support to victims, including victims of racially motivated crime, according to need. However, the attitude of the director of the Frankfurt branch makes it very difficult for ethnic minority victims to obtain help. For example, the victim from Sierra Leone approached the organisation for help. According to the guidelines, he qualified for its services, yet, in interview, the director indicated that she had decided not to support him on the grounds that she disliked him, and that he had once been sentenced to prison. This decision suggests that the organisation has no formal procedures for considering victims' applications for assistance, and that subjective considerations are allowed to determine their outcome.

## The churches

The churches in Germany have traditionally been very involved in multicultural politics. In 1992, the Council of the Protestant Churches in Germany (*Rat der Evangelischen Kirche in Deutschland*) proposed an ecumenical programme to combat xenophobia,[44] because it perceived increasing racism, anti-semitism and xenophobia as a threat to German society. This programme, which has its headquarters in Frankfurt at the Ecumenical Centre (*Ökumenische Centrale*), is to be put into practice in parishes throughout Germany. The programme works in close cooperation with the church initiative *Woche des Ausländischen Mitbürgers* (Inter-Cultural Week for Foreign Residents). The chairman of the programme at the Ecumenical Centre, however, did not mention any specific action to deal with racially motivated crime besides the general anti-discriminatory work.

Apart from the Ecumenical Centre, individual parishes in Frankfurt are very involved in running numerous advisory centres and solidarity groups, with special emphasis on the welfare of refugees and asylum seekers. They offer refugees legal advice and personal help with bureaucratic procedures. Individual parishes are also involved with political solidarity groups.

---

44. Schindehütte, Martin, 'Überwindung von Fremdenfeindlichkeit, Rassismus und Gewalt in Deutschland', in *Ökumenische Rundschau*, Heft 1, January 1995, p.21.

The Jewish and Islamic religious communities also have social welfare offices where they advise members of their communities. However, in Frankfurt they appear not to take part in any large scale, inter-agency measures to combat racially motivated crime.

## CASE STUDIES OF RACIALLY MOTIVATED CRIME[45]

### 1. Hate-letters to Dr Michel Friedmann

Dr Michel Friedmann is a well known public figure and politician in Germany, who is the frequent target of xenophobic and racist threats. He holds a number of public positions, of which the most prominent are:

- Member of the Board of Directors of the Central Council of Jews in Germany (*Zentralrat der Juden in Deutschland*)

- Alderman of the Jewish Congregation in Frankfurt (*Jüdische Gemeinde*)

- Councillor on Frankfurt City Council

- Member of Parliament for the CDU.

In his position as a Jewish MP, Dr Friedmann receives a large number of letters every day. Among these are a number of defamatory or threatening hate-letters. Dr Friedmann is usually not himself interested in taking legal action against the writers of these letters. However, as the amount of racist hate-mail Dr Friedmann receives is very large, the police and public prosecutor's office, in cooperation with Dr Friedmann, have introduced a standard procedure for processing such mail. This case is a very good example of inter-agency cooperation between the police, the public prosecutor's office and the victim. Similar procedures exist for other public figures, such as Ignatz Bubis (Chairman of the Central Council of Jews in Germany).

When the frequency of racist hate-mail to Dr Friedmann increased substantially, the police called a case conference with the public prosecutor and Dr Friedmann. Even if the victim is not interested in taking legal action against the perpetrators, the state has a legal obligation to prosecute certain types of offences. At the case conference, all the participants agreed on a procedure whereby Dr Friedmann would collect all the letters and pass them on regularly to the police. The police would initially assess the letters and then decide whether further legal action was necessary and whether there was any imminent danger to Dr Friedmann. A standard procedure was introduced to process the cases in a clear and comprehensible way. First, the police instituted permanent preliminary proceedings for offences with an anti-semitic background (*ständiges Ermittlungsverfahren mit antisemitischem Hintergrund zum Nachteil Dr Friedmann*) against Dr Friedmann. Secondly, a

---

45. Based predominantly on information from the public prosecutor's archive, interviews and press information.

standard form was drawn up to help the individual officer dealing with the case to assess the situation. The form contains information on the background of the case and a list of headings under which the offence might be categorised. This list helps the individual officer to decide which offence was committed and whether to pass the case on.[46] The investigating officer then has to decide whether further criminal proceedings are justified. If not, the letter is filed by the police without any further action. However, if there is sufficient reason to suspect that a punishable offence has been committed, the case, with a report on the police action to date, is passed on to the public prosecutor's office. The preliminary information helps the public prosecutor to assess the case and speeds up the processing of the information.

### 2. Two Germans beat up a man from Sierra Leone

This is a case where all the statutory agencies agreed that the incident was racially motivated. The attack was accordingly treated as being more severe than comparable incidents without a racial motivation. The case was also processed very quickly at all stages of the investigation and trial. Only the question of victim support was neglected, leading to substantial material and emotional damage for the victim.

The victim, a man from Sierra Leone, sat on a bench in a park talking to a homeless person. Two young white German men approached the victim and asked him for a cigarette. When he told them that he did not have any cigarettes, they started to abuse him verbally. They told him to 'go back to his hut in Africa' and called him a 'nigger'. When the victim did not react to the abuse, the first offender asked his friend whether he should beat up the victim or not. The second offender replied, 'Beat him up, if you want to, he is only a nigger!'

The first offender then brutally attacked the victim, and beat him up so badly that the man sustained multiple injuries including a broken jaw and severe bruises. During the attack, a number of witnesses tried to intervene, but were threatened by the second offender who told them not to interfere, unless they wanted to be beaten up too. He also used neo-Nazi slogans, such as the greeting 'Heil Hitler'. The two offenders simply walked away after the victim lost consciousness, moments before the police arrived at the scene. They searched for the offenders but were unable to track them down.

The statutory agencies reacted very swiftly. The police immediately established a special unit within the CID with sole responsibility for the case, and the city council issued several statements condemning the attack and offering a reward of 10,000 DM for any information leading to the apprehension of the offenders. The public prosecution service decided to follow the city council's step and added a further reward of 5000 DM.[47] Finally, the

---

46. The list contains the following sections of the penal code: 126, 130, 131, 185, 241, and furthermore leaves some room for other sections which might additionally apply.

47. The reason given for offering an additional reward during internal discussion of the case was the 'optical effect'. The public prosecutor responsible for this area of work expressed the view that it would damage the reputation of the public prosecution service not to take part in the reward offer.

regional and national press were informed, and the case was extensively reported. Significantly, the one fact which could so easily have undermined the case in the public perception was not reported: the victim did not give his correct name initially, and pretended to be a different person. This was because he no longer had the right of abode in Germany, that is, he was an illegal immigrant. The victim's real identity was quickly discovered, but neither the press nor any of the statutory agencies gave this much prominence.

Two weeks after the attack, the two perpetrators were identified with the help of three witnesses who recognised one of them from police photographs of known right-wingers. During subsequent questioning by the police, one of the offenders admitted to belonging to a group of skinheads, and maintained that 'Foreigners should be beaten up if they don't behave like German citizens.'

He was also a member of the right-wing group Jungsturm. In a written analysis of the interrogation, the responsible police officer still expresses doubts about the xenophobic motivation of the attack. He is convinced that a verbal argument provoked the physical attack and was therefore the main cause of the incident. However, in the indictment drawn up four weeks later by the public prosecution service, the xenophobic motivation was maintained as a fact. The two men were accused of grievous bodily harm (section 223) and the second offender, who is still an adolescent, was also accused of wearing a symbol from a former Nazi organisation (section 86). During the trial, only the social worker who was looking after the adolescent offender doubted that the young man had strong xenophobic tendencies. Furthermore, she claimed that he had already shown remorse by applying to attend an anti-discrimination seminar and by leaving Jungsturm. The court did not accept this view and both perpetrators were sentenced to one year and six months in prison. These sentences were quite severe: the public prosecution service had only asked for one year for the first offender, and for eight months on probation and a fine for the second. The public prosecutor maintained that the verdict reflected the racial motivation of the perpetrators, as cases of grievous bodily harm normally carry lighter sentences.

However, despite the willingness of the statutory agencies to treat the case as a racial attack, the victim was unable to obtain support from the victim support agency Der Weisse Ring, as our interview with the director and talks with SOS-Rassismus showed. Most people who had any contact with the victim said that he was 'a difficult person'. The procedures used in this area need to be reviewed and revised to ensure that personal opinions do not lead to total neglect of a victim's needs.

### 3. (i) Moroccan man allegedly beaten up by four police officers

### (ii) Police officers suspended from duty after an attack on an ethnic minority suspect

These two cases are examples of the investigation of police racism in Frankfurt. The police force have adopted a general policy that allegations of racist or xenophobic attacks by police officers should be dealt with quickly and carefully. However, this policy is not consistently implemented.

The first incident took place in Frankfurt in October 1992. The victim, a resident of Frankfurt of Moroccan origin, was stopped by four police officers on the street. The officers wanted to check the identity papers of the victim and three other ethnic minority men. The account of the events differs widely between the police on the one hand and the victim and his witness on the other hand.

*The police version.* The police officers claimed that the victim used threatening behaviour towards the officers and that they therefore had to use physical force in order to calm him down. The officers subsequently arrested him and brought him to the police station where he collapsed. The officers claimed that he suffered from an epileptic fit and sustained some injuries in a fall when he lost consciousness. An ambulance was called and the victim had to stay in hospital for nine days.

*The victim's version.* The victim offered a different description. He claimed that he was on his way home after work, when suddenly he and his friend (the witness) were stopped by the four officers. When he demanded an explanation for the check, he was immediately attacked and subsequently pushed into a police van. There, he alleged, he was verbally abused as 'a shitty foreigner', kicked in the testicles and struck in the face. At the police station the officers asked for his asylum papers. When the victim explained that he was legally resident in Germany, one officer allegedly remarked to his colleague, 'You'll be in trouble'. The victim maintained that he collapsed as a result of the prior maltreatment and the doctor who treated him supported his doubts that his injuries were sustained during his fall.

A formal complaint was lodged by the victim's wife the following day, and legal proceedings were initiated by the police two days later. The public prosecution service was informed 19 days later. It took four weeks for the public prosecution service to ask the police to interrogate the officers concerned, and about three weeks after that, all the officers had returned written statements. It is obvious that the officers did not make their statements without prior consultation, as some of them were identically worded. The officers also brought charges against the victim of obstructing an officer in the performance of his duties (*Widerstand gegen die Staatsgewalt*).

The public prosecution service decided to investigate the charges against the victim first before starting the investigation into possible police misconduct. The case against the victim was closed because of the trifling nature of the offence (*wegen Geringfügigkeit eingestellt*) in August 1993, ten months after the initial incident.

The four officers were only interrogated by the public prosecution service in December 1993 and February 1994, one year and three months after the incident. The witness for the victim was interrogated again in July 1994, one year and nine months after the incident.

In February 1995 the victim's lawyer asked the public prosecution service to speed up the case. Finally, in March 1995 the case was abandoned by the public prosecution service because '... it is impossible to decide on the truth as irrefutable evidence from any side is not available'.

The case is an example of how a thorough investigation of alleged police racism was effectively made impossible because of the slow and reluctant processing of the case by the police and public prosecution service. However, there are also examples of cases involving such allegations which were successfully handled in Frankfurt. In October 1994 another victim of North African origin was beaten up by three police officers. This time, a fourth officer who witnessed the attack reported the incident to his superior. The accused officers were immediately suspended from duty, even before the investigation was closed. The allegations were proved to be correct, and the officers were arrested and are currently awaiting trial. The Minister for the Interior in Hesse has asked for an independent investigation of possible negligence by the police departments responsible for the accused officers.

In this case, the police and public prosecution service reacted swiftly and without any delay. However, the guidelines for handling such cases should be reviewed and revised to eliminate any possibility of covering up racist incidents within the police force.

## 4. Attempted manslaughter

This is a case where a racial motivation was assumed by the police on the grounds of external factors. Neither the victim nor any of the witnesses expressed the view that the attack was racially motivated. The classification of the case as 'racially motivated' despite the lack of any obvious evidence from the actual attack indicates the amount of care the police and public prosecution service take in order to avoid underestimating possible racial factors.

One afternoon, a conflict arose between a number of people drinking beer at a refreshment kiosk. A German man got into an argument with an Italian man. When the dispute appeared to be over, the German left. However, he soon returned and, without prior warning, shot the Italian twice in the abdomen. The German was finally overpowered by a number of witnesses, and the Italian, who was critically wounded, was taken to hospital, where he had to undergo an emergency operation. The offender was arrested by the police. During the police examination the offender claimed that the victim had called him a 'Nazi pig'. The police also discovered that the offender was a member of the Deutsche Volksunion, a right-wing, nationalist party with strong xenophobic tendencies. Furthermore, the offender had a number of previous convictions, including one for a violent attack on another Italian national. On the basis of this information, the police questioned the offender about his attitude to foreigners and ethnic minorities. He admitted to having problems with foreigners, and claimed to have had a number of disputes with his non-German neighbours.

Although neither of the witnesses nor the victim himself voiced any suspicion that the shooting might have been racially motivated, the factors mentioned above were sufficient for the police to classify the attack as possibly xenophobic. When the case was passed on to the public prosecution service, the public prosecutor agreed to treat the case as racially motivated, subject to further investigation, and duly informed the Ministry of Justice about it, as laid down in the regulations on racially motivated crime. The offender was sentenced to five years in prison, which, according to the public prosecutor, was a comparatively severe sentence for such a crime.

### 5. Alleged racist arson attack on the flat of a Jordanian family

This is a case where the police and public prosecution service decided to treat an incident as racially motivated even though they had strong doubts about the motivation from the beginning. The press, too, reported extensively on the attack as long as it was suspected to be racially motivated.

A woman from Jordan reported several cases of arson to the police. The police suspected that the arson attacks were self-inflicted, but decided to treat the case as a racially motivated crime in order to avoid accusations of police negligence. Several anti-racist groups decided to support the victim's family, for example, by posting guards outside the victim's house to prevent further attacks. The local and regional newspapers reported regularly on the case. However, the police's suspicion of self-inflicted damage was quickly confirmed – the victim had committed the arson 'attacks' herself. This discovery was not reported extensively by the press, and was also dealt with quietly by the judicial agencies. The response of the media and the statutory agencies, who were concerned to prevent the possibility of collective defamation of all victims of racist attacks, was exemplary. In the aftermath of the wave of xenophobic attacks, intense media attention on the fraudulent nature of this incident could have led to more accusations of 'self-inflicted' attacks. For example, suspicion of an 'internal Turkish conflict' was discussed nationwide in the spectacular case of the Solingen murder – a suspicion based only on an anonymous fax sent to the judge which soon proved to be incorrect. In Frankfurt, the Jordanian 'victim' was finally accused of arson and sentenced to two years and nine months in prison.

## CONCLUSIONS

The dramatic increase in racist and xenophobic attacks in Germany has led to the common realisation that both state and society have to respond to the challenge of racism and xenophobia with determination. The government has issued strong guidelines for the relevant statutory agencies, has started a number of anti-racist initiatives, and has amended certain parts of the law in order to ensure effective prosecution of perpetrators and indemnification for victims of such attacks. The police and judicial agencies hold key positions in the fight against racism and xenophobia, and it is their response which largely determines the credibility of a country's efforts to overcome racist and xenophobic tendencies. The police represent state authority, and are especially responsible for protecting the fundamental values of a democratic society.

It is not enough, however, to assess political commitment at the national level alone. The federal nature of Germany makes it necessary to pay special attention to the implementation of national policies at the local level. Our analysis of the situation in Frankfurt shows that all the relevant agencies are strongly committed to combating racially motivated crime and have taken several commendable measures to prevent and tackle racist and xenophobic incidents. For example:

- The police video film on emergency calls and the leaflets in ethnic minority languages produced in cooperation with the DMA and KAV.

- The introduction of special community officers for the ethnic minority population.

- The regular meetings between the police, the DMA and the ethnic minority population.

- The introduction of Commissioners for Foreigners in the police force.

- The new opportunities for members of ethnic minorities to enter the police force.

- The introduction of the KAV as a directly elected body for the ethnic minority population.

- The introduction of special investigation units within the police force.

- The allocation of specific responsibility for racist and xenophobic crimes to one public prosecutor.

- The introduction of special racist incident forms by the prosecution service to facilitate statistical analysis of racist and xenophobic crime.

- The cooperation between the police and the public prosecutors, which helps to accelerate the processing of cases and ensure consistent procedures.

Notwithstanding these achievements, problems still remain, and improvements are needed in certain areas. The evidence from the study in Frankfurt suggests that there is a discrepancy between the political commitment of the relevant statutory agencies and the actual implementation of anti-racist policies. All the institutions which were investigated had made considerable efforts in the field and set up many convincing initiatives against racially motivated crime. However, most institutions introduced anti-racist procedures hastily as an immediate reaction to the increase in racially motivated crime. This lack of long-term planning becomes apparent in a number of structural weaknesses. For example:

- The question of monitoring anti-racist policies is severely neglected both by the police and the public prosecution service.

- Both agencies need to institute obligatory control mechanisms in order to avoid unnecessary delays and negligence when processing cases of racially motivated crime.

- The police should introduce separate racist incident forms in order to avoid inconsistent registration procedures and to make it easier for officers to process cases. At present the decision to enter potential racial motivation in a case on the incident form depends solely on the officer handling the case.

- The DMA should introduce a standard system for recording racially motivated incidents – the current system is very haphazard and does not allow for thorough evaluation of such cases.

- Procedures for dealing with racial attacks committed by police officers need to be reviewed and revised. An unbiased investigation cannot be guaranteed if the colleagues of suspected officers are responsible for investigating the case.

- The procedures for ensuring victim support need urgent attention. Although the statutory agencies are obliged to inform the victim about victim support agencies, they very rarely do so, and in Frankfurt non-governmental organisations have taken over this responsibility. However, even the non-governmental organisations cannot be relied upon to treat all victims of racially motivated crime consistently.

- The institutionalisation of inter-agency cooperation will ensure a more coordinated approach to racially motivated crime and less reliance on the individuals working in the field.

Despite these weaknesses, the example of Frankfurt shows that the combination of a strong political commitment to combating racially motivated crime with the implementation of anti-racist policies has produced some effective countermeasures. Frankfurt's agencies measure up well against the recommendations of the police and criminal justice report of the Kahn Committee. But, as many of the interviewees said, more dialogue at European level will help all agencies to improve their policies and procedures.

# APPENDIX 1

**Cases of racially motivated crime recorded by the public prosecutor in Frankfurt am Main**

| Month | Xenophobic attack (XA) | Right-wing attack (RW) | Cases carried over from previous month |
|---|---|---|---|
| January | 2 | 6 | 70(xa), 50 (rw) |
| February | 2 | 3 | 71 (xa), 56 (rw) |
| March | 4 | 6 | 73 (xa), 59 (rw) |
| April | 0 | 4 | no longer stated |
| May | 0 | 6 | |
| June | 2 | 3 | |
| July | 1 | 1 | |
| August | 1 | 3 | |
| September | 3 | 10 | |
| October | 2 | 6 | |
| November | 4 | 8 | |
| December | 3 | 7 | |
| **Total** | **24** | **63** | |

# REFERENCES

Amnesty International, *Ausländer als Opfer. Polizeiliche Misshandlungen in der Bundesrepublik*, May 1995.

Amt für Multikulturelle Angelegenheiten, *Zweieinhalb Jahre Amt für Multikulturelle Angelegenheiten*, Frankfurt, 1993.

Amt für Statistik, Wahlen und Einwohnerwesen, *Statistische Porträts. Ausländer und Ausländerinnen in Frankfurt am Main*, Frankfurt, 1995.

Beratende Kommission Rassismus und Fremdenfeindlichkeit, *Schlussbericht der Beratenden Kommission*, Bruxelles, 1995.

Bundesministerium des Innern, *Verfassungsschutzbericht 1993*, Bonn, 1994.

Bundesministerium für Arbeit, *Der Staat hilft den Opfern von Gewalttaten*, Bonn, 1994.

Franzke, Bettina, *Die Polizei in Kontakt und Konflikt mit Menschen ausländischer Herkunft*, Frankfurt, 1993.

Frommel, Monika, 'Die Polizei dein Feind und Schläger', in *Die Woche*, 22 September,1994.

Hessisches Landeskriminalamt, *Landeslagebild Fremdenfeindliche Straftaten in Hessen*, 1 January – 31 December 1993, Wiesbaden, 1994.

Hessisches Landeskriminalamt, letter by the director, Mr Timm, where the comprehensive strategy against racially motivated crime is outlined, 27 June 1995.

Hessische Landesregierung, *Bericht über die Umsetzung der politischen Initiativen der Hessischen Landesregierung zur Eindâämmung des Rechtsextremismus und seiner Ursachen*, 1994.

Kommunale Ausländer- und Ausländerinnenvertretung, Jahresbericht 1993, 1. Wahlperiode, Frankfurt, 1993.

Leggewie, Claus, *MultiKulti. Spielregeln für die Vielvölkerrepublik*, Nördlingen, 1990.

Polizei Frankfurt, *Die Ausländerbeauftragten der Frankfurter Polizei*, 1993.

Press and Information Office of the Federal Government, Foreign Affairs Division, *The Situation of Foreigners in Germany. Facts, Analyses, Arguments on Hostility towards Foreigners*, Bonn, 1995.

Schindehütte, Martin, 'Überwindung von Fremdenfeindlichkeit, Rassismus und Gewalt in Deutschland', in *Ökumenische Rundschau*, 1 January 1995.

'Sozialarbeiter sollen vermitteln. Stadt will Konflikt um acht Roma Familien entschärfen', in *Frankfurter Allgemeine Zeitung*, 13 September 1994.

Stadt Frankfurt am Main, Handbuch der Stadtverordnetenversammlung, XIII. Wahlperiode, Frankfurt 1993.

Stadt Frankfurt am Main, *Jahresbericht 1993*, Stadtverordnetenversammlung XIII, Wahlperiode.

*Statistisches Jahrbuch der Stadt*, Frankfurt, 1993.

*Statistisches Jahrbuch Deutscher Gemeinden*, Grosstädte, 1994.

'Video-Clip als Hilfe: Notruf für Ausländer', in *Frankfurter Rundschau*, 20 July 1993.

# CHAPTER THREE

# LYONS

Colette Smith

## INTRODUCTION

This report is based on interviews carried out in Lyons and its suburbs at the end of 1994 and in the first half of 1995. In September 1995 a few more interviews were conducted and the progress of court cases updated whenever possible.

### France, French terminology and the research project

Once the hurdle of finding a working translation for the title of the project was cleared, other obstacles presented themselves. The greatest difficulty was to try to work to guidelines established for a British context which made little or no sense in a French context.

For anyone living in France there are only two kinds of status. A person is either a French national or an alien. This explains why, on the whole, the concept of minorities or the registration of crime under the various ethnic origins of the criminal or the victim is quite alien to French thinking and almost absent from police legal or administrative records.

In France there is no recognition of racially motivated crime. What is recognised by the authorities is crime directed against people who actually are, or are perceived to be, foreigners; and the denial of the rights of immigrants.

The work in the Lyons suburbs was very rewarding and it was unfortunate that more time and space could not be devoted to direct interviews with people from the various minorities on their experience of racial violence. Talking to some of them I found that the very question of what counts as racial violence and hatred is crucial, since it was felt that sometimes the way people look at you is enough to amount to provocation.

Since the completion of the research project depended entirely on the cooperation of the people I interviewed, I have been very lucky. I did not find it difficult to have access to the people I wished to talk to and, on the whole, they were extremely open and frank. I would like to thank them very sincerely. A list of those interviewed can be found on page 96.

## RACIAL COMPOSITION OF THE AREA

Since the research refers to statistics from the Institut National de la Statistique et des Etudes Economiques (INSEE), its definitions of the terms 'alien' and 'immigrant' have been adopted for this study.[1] In the 'alien' category in France, people from the Maghreb (for the most part Moroccans and Algerians[2]) form the largest group. Other ethnic groups include Asians, Turks, Rwandans, Afghans, Romanians and people from former Yugoslavia. These ethnic groups are concentrated in and around the three largest cities in France: Paris, Lyons and Marseilles. This study focuses on Lyons.

The police estimate the population of Lyons at one million inhabitants, not counting smaller towns such as Villefranche, Grigny and Tarrare which are also the responsibility of the Lyons police and which have 30,000, 27,000 and 11,000 inhabitants respectively. A thriving city, long famous for its silk industry and an advanced banking system, Lyons has always attracted a considerable number of foreigners, who eventually stayed in the city. At the end of the nineteenth century immigrant workers in the Lyons region were predominantly male (the main exception being women who came from the USA and UK). In 1888 Monsieur Pradon, Member of Parliament for the Ain *département* (on the doorstep of Lyons) complained of 'an invasion of foreign workers'. These workers came mainly from Italy, Switzerland and Germany. I was often reminded by those I interviewed that, although fully integrated now, and usually strongly anti-immigrant and pro-Le Pen in political conviction, the Italians had suffered serious attacks and had been the butt of xenophobic jibes when they first came to Lyons.

Immigration from the Maghreb goes back to the beginning of this century. Place du Pont has long been the Algerian Muslim quarter of the city, shared with a small Armenian community. Jews from the Maghreb established themselves at about the same time in another old part of the city, Saint Jean and St. Paul. The area has now been rejuvenated and given over to tourists, who reach it via Rue d'Algérie and stroll along the Rue Juiverie.

The First World War introduced women in the Lyons region to the world of paid work. Like women in Britain, they went to work in munition factories and were reluctant to leave their employment at the end of a war which left 1.3 million dead and one million wounded in France. It was French policy at the time to recruit workers from its colonies, in particular from Kabylia (Algeria) and Indo-China, but also from China. In the 1920s France

---

1. An alien: anyone who does not have French nationality. An immigrant: anyone born in a foreign country but living in France – the immigrant may either remain a foreigner or become a French citizen.

2. The case of the Algerians is perhaps the most complex and is intrinsically linked to the colonial history of that country and the various moments of French industrialisation. First, Algerians were encouraged to come to France as immigrant workers, then by virtue of the status of the colony they either became French nationals or were foreign residents. Following the independence of Algeria most chose Algerian nationality, but those Algerians who fought alongside the French (Harkis) and were on the side of 'Algérie française', opted for French status.

became the first country of immigration, ahead of the USA and Germany.[3] Inward movement peaked in 1929.

In 1931 the proportions of immigrant workers in industrial suburbs such as Givors, Vénissieux, Vaulx en Velin were 44 per cent, 40 per cent and 55 per cent respectively. In the same year, a group of working women complained that their jobs were jeopardised by the employment of foreign workers and appealed for protection. In 1931, immigrants represented 6.6 per cent of the whole population of France and 7.4 per cent of the working population.[4]

As well as immigrant workers 'invited' by the French government, refugees from turbulent regimes came to the Lyons region. Family groups and even village groups came from Spain, Russia, Armenia and Poland.

The economic crisis of 1931 was followed by a change of policy. From 1932 foreign workers were not only discouraged from coming to France but encouraged to return home. In the census of 1936 foreigners represented only 5.3 per cent of the total population and 6.1 per cent of the 'active' population.[5] With the economic crisis, a wave of xenophobia swept the Lyons region and was directed, in 1934, against the Italians. Their community was large, they ran Italian language classes for their children and had political associations whose allegiance was to the Italian flag rather than the *tricolore*. They were perceived as resisting integration and were considered a menace.

By the late 1930s women formed a more noticeable proportion of the immigrant population; they came with the men who had found employment. In the 1950s women were encouraged to come to France through a policy of family reunion (*regroupement familial*).

After the Second World War immigration became an imperative for the French government. France needed a workforce but also needed to rebuild its population, decimated by two wars. ONI (l'Office National de l'Immigration) was created in 1945 and was given the responsibility of organising and controlling the recruitment of foreign workers. From the 1950s, the number of foreigners increased, but their countries of origin were different from earlier immigration movements: the numbers from European countries declined while those from the Maghreb and, to a lesser extent, from Turkey, South East Asia and Black Africa increased. In 1974 measures were taken to stop permanent immigration by workers, except for those from the EEC, leading to a fall in the proportion of active foreign workers in France, from 7.4 per cent in 1975 to 6.4 per cent in 1990.

The 1990 census for the Rhône *département* (where Lyons is situated) shows that the proportion of foreigners was higher in this region than in France as a whole. The number of foreigners in the Rhône area peaked in 1975, with the largest group coming from Algeria. By 1990 the number of Portuguese, Italian and Spanish people had decreased considerably, while

---

3. Phillippe Videlier, *Histoire des vagues migratoires en Rhône Alpes*, conference paper, 27 January 1994.

4. *Ibid.*

5. Active population is described in INSEE documents as: working people, unemployed people and, since 1990, young men doing their military service.

the number of Algerians remained much higher than any other group.

The majority of people from ethnic minorities now live in suburbs (*banlieues*) at the periphery of the city, such as Vaulx en Velin, Vénissieux, Villeurbanne (Saint Jean and Mas du Taureau districts) or Bron Parilly. These were built in the middle of nowhere (or almost) during the inter-war years or soon after the Second World War to accommodate a large population of low waged people in social housing (*habitation à loyer modéré* (HLM)). They have very few local amenities such as shops, cinemas and even, in some cases, schools or sports grounds, and live in the high-rise tower blocks that were erected in the 1960s, such as La Duchère or Les Minguettes.

It was in these suburbs that the first serious incidents introduced new phrases to the French language such as *les banlieues chaudes* (suburban trouble spots). After the shooting by the police of some young Maghrébins in Les Minguettes, the impetus, following the famous march of December 1983,[6] was to create a ministry responsible for the problems of the city. In 1995 this was in the hands of Simone Weil. It was also in the mid-1980s that associations such as SOS Racisme,[7] with its campaign *touche pas à mon pote* (leave my mate alone), and JALB (Jeunes Arabes de Lyon et des Banlieues) were set up, as well as the now defunct ASTI. These associations were integrationist[8] in spirit, and often still are (SOS Racisme in particular). They campaign for the rights of people from ethnic minorities, organising functions and supporting victims of racially motivated crimes by helping them to take their cases to court.

## THE LAW ON RACIALLY MOTIVATED CRIME

Article 2 of the French Constitution states:

> France is a Republic, indivisible, secular, democratic and social. It shall ensure the equality of all citizens before the law, without distinction of origin, race or religion. It shall respect all beliefs.

The Commission Consultative des Droits de l'Homme (an official body based in the Prime Minister's office) publishes an annual table of racially motivated crime and records the various crimes covered by the *Code Pénal* (Criminal Code), its amendments and revisions, under nine headings:

- racial defamation

- racial injury

---

6. Marche pour l'égalité et contre le racisme. The march started from Les Minguettes district of Lyons, and the participants, who numbered 100,000 at their destination in Paris, covered 2,000 kilometres on foot. It is worth noting that the now famous (or infamous) tower blocks of Les Minguettes were eventually blown up in the late 1980s.

7. SOS Racisme was created in 1985.

8. Not to be mistaken for the French term *intégriste* which means fundamentalist.

- racial incitement

- desecration of burial grounds

- apologia of crime

- crime against humanity (introduced after the trials of Klaus Barbie and Paul Touvier)

- exhibitions of illicit insignia

- racial discrimination in employment

- racial discrimination in the provision of goods and services.

The criminal code is explicit about the repression of racially motivated crime and goes to great lengths to make sure that the law upholds the rights of the citizen. In spite of such rigorous legislation, there were only 138 convictions for racially motivated crime in 1991 and 111 in 1992; the highest fine in 1991 was 8,800 Ff. and 9,750 Ff in 1992; and the longest penal sentence was 7.4 months in 1991 and 3.6 months in 1992 [9]

Everyone interviewed for this study agreed that it was extremely difficult to bring claims of discrimination or racially motivated crime before the courts, because of the problems with evidence. For example, it was very hard to get a complaint of racial discrimination in the workplace registered, and next to impossible to find witnesses or people ready to testify. Furthermore, there were the financial implications of bringing cases, since legal aid amounts to only 900 Ff. The 1985 law, which allows anti-racist associations to press charges in cases of violent crime against people from ethnic minorities when '... crimes of violence have been committed against a person because of his/her national origin, his/her belonging, whether it is true or imagined, to an ethnic group, a race or a given religion', has certainly helped, and organisations such as SOS Racisme, JALB and CRARDA (see pp 74-5) have used these powers. Some of those interviewed blamed the magistrates for 'blatant racism', but the French judicial system has made several efforts to alert practitioners to the scope of the law and to advise them on initiatives they should take to uphold it. The latest guide, *Guide des lois antiracistes*, was published by the French Ministry of Justice in autumn 1994.

Between 1972 and 1989 successive Ministers of Justice have issued no fewer than six articles of recommendation to the courts in order to alert them and to recommend vigilance in the application of anti-discriminatory legislation. The Circular of 1989, for example, which recalled the various powers at the disposal of the judiciary to intervene in the fight against racism, reminded magistrates of the Public Ministry that it was up to them to '... take the initiative in judicial action without waiting for the victim or an association to be obliged to act'.

---

9. La documentation française, *Aspects de la Criminalité et de la Délinquance ...*, Paris, 1993.

This series of recommendations was followed by the law of 13 July 1990, which brought three new elements to the judicial apparatus: reinforcement of the various sentences; a new category of crime – crime against humanity; and new prerogatives for associations.[10]

Successive Ministers of Justice have on the whole been aware of the costs of court proceedings and have often issued strong recommendations that the financial hurdle should not be so prohibitive as to deter victims of racially motivated offences from taking legal action.[11]

## Views from the legal profession

A Lyonnais barrister who represents victims of racially motivated crime summed up the situation in the following way: '... very firm legislation which contrasts totally with what really happens'. She maintained that, '...at the two ends of the spectrum anomalies occur'. For instance, illegal immigrants who have managed to stay in France – and this is not terribly difficult – will (because of the strict laws on education and welfare) receive help from statutory bodies and benevolent institutions. Their children will go to school, and the local authorities will provide housing for their families, who will also be entitled to benefits such as RMI (basic social security), and child benefit.

Although she produced no evidence, this barrister's view was that, in a case of grievous bodily harm inflicted on a Maghrébin, for example, the culprit may be sent to prison for up to five years; whereas grievous bodily harm inflicted by a Maghrébin is punishable by imprisonment for between ten and 20 years. For example, Monsieur Kouskoussa, the victim of a vicious racial attack, was shot in the neck in front of his flat. He is now confined to a wheel chair and lives in a hostel for incurable people, shaking at the thought that his assailant was released after serving a very short sentence.

In this barrister's experience, a racial motive is very seldom taken into account. This was also confirmed by Judge Seyz, who said that 'racial motivation is not considered to be an aggravating circumstance', and that in most cases of racial discrimination, in employment for example, the stumbling block was the question of evidence and witnesses.

Isabelle Passet, a *juge d'instruction* at the Tribunal de Lyon, thought that racially motivated crimes mostly go unpunished. In her experience of over ten years, there have been no more than ten convictions for racial crime as defined by the French judicial system. Most of the cases she hears involving people from the various minorities involve accusations of low level crimes, belying public perception (fostered by extreme right-wing propaganda) of a 'criminal class' of immigrants. The judge thought that heavy sentences were handed out for crimes that seem rather petty in order to placate public opinion, and that pressure was put on the courts to hear such cases as quickly as

---

10. La documentation française, *La Lutte contre le Racisme et la Xénophobie*, Paris 1991.

11. Circular of May 1987.

possible, pushing much graver criminal offences to the back of the queue.[12] She stressed that present French policies towards foreigners and asylum seekers were putting an enormous strain both on administrative and judicial resources and on the police, with the main emphasis being the 'criminalisation of foreigners in general and in particular of parents whose children have a nationality different from their own'.

On the treatment of racially motivated crime in court, Isabelle Passet made two important points: first, that a procedural system does exist, but is badly used, and secondly, that victims are not adequately protected and are therefore fearful and hesitate to bring their case to court. She also thought that the weight of evidence of racial motivation in violent crimes was 'diluted or completely unrecognised' when judgements were given. On the question of victim support and neighbourhood crime, she felt that the *Maisons de Justice* were doing a very good job. She also praised the work of associations such as CRARDA and SOS Racisme, which initiate court cases.

## Les Maisons de Justice

Most neighbourhood crime is dealt with by the *Maisons de Justice*. Lyons has four *Maisons de Justice*, all in the populous suburbs of the city: Villeurbanne, the Huitième (Eighth) Arrondissement, Bron, and Vaulx en Velin. They deal with minor offences, and the judgements delivered by the Magistrats de Parquet come under two categories:

- *affaire classée* (the case has been heard and no more will happen, there is no mention on the individual's *casier judiciaire* (police record), or

- *classement sous conditions* (social workers and probation officers will be required to intervene).

The victim's case has the best chance of being heard in the category of a *classement sous conditions*. In her interview, the judge felt that this was the nearest example of victim support she could find (except for Villeurbanne Information Femmes Famille, an association which deals mainly with violence towards women). This was because the victim usually gets a chance to meet his or her assailants during the probation period, and to receive compensation from them.

Another judge said that all the cases he heard were connected with the expulsion of illegal immigrants, and that this was where the 'Pasqua effect' could be observed. The extreme vigilance of police searches for illegal immigrants exacerbated the difficulties faced by young Maghrébins who had not yet opted for French nationality. They were arrested along with 'genuine foreigners', asylum seekers and illegal immigrants. (By the end of the research period, an all-out campaign against illegal immigration was in full swing, as

---

12. One case mentioned was that of two youths (of Maghrébin origin) who stole a tool box from a bus and were sent to prison for two months. They had no previous convictions.

well as a hunt for the suspected terrorists who had planted bombs in Paris and Lyons.)

The fate of people arrested by the police and suspected of being illegal immigrants is finally decided by the Prefect, but the judicial authorities must be consulted first.

## THE ROLE OF CHURCHES, ASSOCIATIONS AND LOCAL INITIATIVES

All of the following associations seek to help minorities with a variety of problems, and some of them act as *partie civile* in court cases.

### CIMADE

At the time of this study, the main concern of CIMADE (Comité Inter Mouvements auprès des Evacués), a church based organisation, was the state authorities' treatment of foreigners (or those perceived as such) and asylum seekers, rather than racially motivated crime.

The association originated in south west France in 1939, when a group of practising Protestants decided to visit internment camps in the region. The group organised escape routes and safe houses for Jews in the 1940s, supported decolonisation in the 1950s, and came to concentrate in the 1970s on the problems of refugees and immigrants. CIMADE is a national association with many active branches. It works with the ecumenical Council of Churches, the federation of French Protestant churches, the Orthodox Church in France and various Catholic and non-denominational organisations. The head of the Lyons branch is a Protestant minister, Jean Costil. Father Delorme, a Catholic priest whose name was continually mentioned in the course of this study, was originally part of the CIMADE team. Officially attached to a Catholic church, he was the only person interviewed who felt that the churches and other associations were making a great mistake in not being more open and welcoming to Islam.

The main activities of the churches are to give practical help to people in great need and to provide legal advice and support to refugees, asylum seekers and immigrants. They run reception centres and provide emergency accommodation for immigrants and asylum seekers, but this is inadequate to the urgent demand for living space. For example the Catholic-run Foyer de Notre Dame Sans Abri (Our Lady of the Homeless) houses in some cases three generations of the same family, although it was intended to provide only temporary accommodation.

### SOS Racisme

SOS Racisme is a national organisation whose membership is open to all: French citizens and foreigners. It has many local branches, including one in Lyons where a Muslim woman, Houria Chikhaoui, is President. SOS Racisme can be a *partie civile* in court cases, but the expense of going to court is becoming prohibitive.

I was told that the main difficulty in cases of racially motivated crime was one of procedure, since it is the victim who must lodge a complaint: only then can the association help the individual. The racial motive was seldom taken into account when convictions were obtained. In the views of those I spoke to, direct action, including large demonstrations and the denunciation of racially motivated crime, was the only course left when minority groups' interests were threatened.

Public campaigning is a major part of SOS Racisme's work, but it also helps individuals with problems of residence in France, and organises street education and some contacts with schools.

## CRARDA

CRARDA (Comité Rhodanien d'Accueil des Réfugiés et Défense du Droit d'Asile, that is Rhône Regional Committee for the Reception of Refugees and the Defence of the Right of Asylum) is a state-financed organisation dealing entirely with asylum seekers and immigrants awaiting French status. It runs two accommodation centres where it helps people to apply for benefit. It also fights repatriations with a small number of dedicated barristers. Legal aid is obtainable but is quite inadequate to cover the costs.

CRARDA's director said it was very difficult indeed to bring any action under the heading of racial discrimination. Practices at all levels, by the magistrates, police and public prosecutors, militated against the application of the 1972 anti-discrimination law. He was very critical of unpunished racism, not only against immigrants but also against Jews, who had suffered attacks as well as desecration of cemeteries. The creation of a *Cellule Anti-Raciste* (anti-racist think tank) under the authority of the Prefect had been completely ineffective: its members had met only once and that was over a year earlier.

## JALB

JALB (Association des Jeunes Arabes de Lyon et Banlieues, that is Association of Young Arabs in Lyons and its Suburbs) is a local organisation of young Arabs jointly financed by national funds (FAS), the city of Lyons and the *communes* (banlieues). It provides information and advice, supports or initiates direct action, and acts as *partie civile* in court cases. It has often acted in cases where it believed a charge of racism should be made, but this charge has never been upheld, even in the more blatant cases.

As JALB sees it, the main problem for young Maghrébins lies in French immigration law. Many of the young fail to obtain French nationality because they do not apply in time or do not want to approach the local authorities (*Préfecture*). Those born in France often believe that they do not need to apply, that they are already French.

Another problem, apparently a recent one, has been complaints about being refused places in schools.

## Agora

Agora is based in Vaulx en Velin, a working-class suburb with a largely Maghrébin population and a communist local administration. Agora members are drawn from the local community and, it was said, had no desire for personal promotion. I was unable to obtain information about how many members there were or their names, and those I interviewed were unwilling to talk much about their aims and activities, except to describe their educational work with young children locally.

Like other associations, Agora is state-funded. It has premises in a block of HLM (social housing managed by the local council). It does not fight court cases. I was given no direct answers to questions about racially motivated crime, but told instead that all the problems of the present generation derived from the hoodwinking of the older Maghrébin generation by the French and from an educational system which failed to make use of their talent. One said integration of Algerians in France was impossible as long as France did not recognise the genocide it had committed in Algeria.

This group put forward its own candidates in the local elections.

## Tiberius Claudius

This recently formed group brings together people active in other associations, such as CIMADE, CRARDA and ALPIL, in cooperation with barristers. It helps asylum seekers with their court cases, and did so in the case of the Romanian Gypsies described below (see p. 81).

## Agir Ensemble pour les Droits de l'Homme

Agir Ensemble (Joint Action for Human Rights) is mainly concerned with work at international level. In Lyons, it joined other associations in their declaration of vigilance during the election campaign (see p. 88).

## La Ligue des Droits de l'Homme

La Ligue des Droits de l'Homme (The Human Rights League) has been established in Lyons for a long time and has recently become active again. It was one of the associations involved in the declaration of vigilance.

## LICRA

LICRA (La Ligue Contre Racisme et Anti-Sémitisme, that is League against Racism and Anti-semitism) deals with anti-semitic attacks. Like La Ligue des Droits de L'Homme, LICRA is a national organisation which depends entirely on voluntary helpers. In Lyons these are mainly active retired gentlemen.

## MRAP

MRAP (Mouvement contre le Racisme et pour l'Amitié entre les Peuples, that is Movement against Racism and for Friendship between Peoples) is a national organisation, very active and well known in Paris. Its workers include some who were in the Resistance against the Nazis. The local branch in Lyons appears to be mainly concerned with the problems of Maghrébins.

### Centre d'Animation de Saint Jean: a local initiative

Saint Jean is a suburb of Lyons, next to Vaulx en Velin. Its population is diverse and mostly poor. There are three blocks of social housing run by Sans Abri, several social housing estates and two Gypsy settlements. Completed in 1968, this social housing at first had no shops or schools. Under pressure from the inhabitants, facilities were improved in the 1970s and early 1980s. A youth club was provided, but was vandalised – a fire followed a squat – and then put out of action altogether (by the 'lost generation' of local young people, according to the centre's director). The Centre d'Animation now serves as part youth club, part evening institute, part drop-in centre. It gives direct help to children, preparing the youngest for their first schools, giving out-of-school help to older ones, and eventually helping school-leavers and older adults to look for jobs. Unemployment in the area is very high, and many local people live on RMI.

Asked to sum up the main problems in the area, the director said 'exclusion', by which he meant dire poverty. He described the achievement of the Centre as *brassage*, a term interestingly different from 'integration', since it implies the mixing together of people of different origins, ages and incomes.

## COURT CASES

The following summaries of court cases are based on documents and interviews with barristers and members of organisations which helped the victims either to prepare their defence in court or to initiate court proceedings.

### 1. Yahyaoui and Boubakar, 23 March 1993

Two Tunisian youths playing truant from a class at the local secondary school were walking along the street when they met a French youth. One of the young Tunisians felt that the French youth was looking at him in a funny way and decided to go up to him. Two of the French youth's friends came up and a brawl ensued involving five youths. In the scuffle the French youth's *blouson* (jacket) was torn. A police car turned up and the French youths decided to report the incident. At that point the main complaint concerned the torn *blouson*. The police decided to look for the Tunisian youths. Seeing the police vehicle, one of the two Tunisian boys threw away a watch in the gutter under the police car. He maintained that during the brawl the French youth's watch had fallen to the ground, that he had seen it and picked it up.

The police described the case in these words: 'two individuals stopped and attacked a youth in the street in order to rob him'. Of previously good character, with a very acceptable school report and support from his teachers and headteacher (who later requested that the youth be allowed some supervised custody in order to take his exams), Yahaoui was sentenced to six months' imprisonment with five months' suspended sentence in 1993. An appeal was lodged and by the autumn of 1994, the two youths were still awaiting the tribunal's decision. One of them was taking exams and living an almost normal life, according to the barrister following the case. The other youth was more elusive and the barrister expressed concern about the effect of the case on his behaviour. One immediate difficulty for both youths was that, under French nationality laws, they have to show exemplary behaviour for five years before they can apply for French nationality (should they decide to do so).

The appeal court decided on 1 December 1994 to set the penalty at one year in prison with six months' suspended sentence and denial of civic rights for five years.

## 2. Khireddine

This case involved the constitution of a dossier for a young woman requesting territorial asylum. Of Algerian parentage, she was brought up in France, and her brothers and sisters lived in a Lyons suburb. After qualifying in France, Khireddine was offered work in Algeria and went to live there. She is now threatened in Algeria. A dossier of documents translated by Inter Service Migrants[13] supports this, but she was only granted a visa, issued in Nantes, which allowed her to return to France for 40 days. The appeal on her behalf was initiated by a local barrister, but it was not dealt with by the court but by the Préfecture du Rhône, Direction de la Réglementation, Third Bureau.

The interesting point here is the power of the police in all cases of nationality and asylum. This point was emphasised and deplored by the two judges interviewed during this research. They both felt that since the Pasqua regulations, the decision on whether or not to grant territorial asylum is in fact taken by the Préfecture. Whereas before Pasqua the role of the judiciary was compulsory, it is now only consultative. Although all cases must be heard in court, in reality the decision to expel a foreigner is taken by the Prefect, who always refuses right of entry, said the judge.

## 3. Youbi and Madaci, 21 March 1994

This is perhaps the most famous case of all. After a demonstration in Lyons at which the police were pelted with stones, some police officers said they recognised the youths who had attacked them. Two older youths (both Algerians) were arrested, and a much younger girl was released after interview. Youbi and Madaci said in their deposition that Youbi had gone to visit his sister in hospital, that he had met Madaci and the younger girl in town but had not taken part in the demonstration.

Although later presented as no angels by the police and the press,

---

13. A long established organisation with a reliable section dealing with translation.

neither youth had a previous conviction and they were set free by the tribunal. As they came out of the tribunal, they were arrested by the Police des Etrangers under instructions from the Préfet de Police in Lyons. They were served with an immediate expulsion order (*un arrêt d'expulsion en urgence absolue*), and were deported to Algeria on 24 March 1994, a country which neither of them knew.

Following a press campaign, representations from organisations such as CIMADE, active support from SOS Racisme, and a youth demonstration in the streets of Lyons, the two youths were brought back to France.

The result has been absolutely catastrophic for Madaci, who was convicted of another crime committed after his return to France. He returned to France to a divided family: he had to leave Lyons to go and live with his father in a small country town and things took a turn for the worse for him. Youbi on the other hand seems to have survived the ordeal and his lawyer is optimistic: she thinks that the worst is over and that with the solid backing of his family he will be all right.

The case brought by the police for the original stone throwing incident came before the Lyons courts on 30 May 1995. The police felt under attack, since the discrepancies between their report and the deposition in court were too great for the judge to ignore. The prosecuting magistrate requested a six months' suspended sentence and three years' suspension of civic rights. The court gave its final decision on 4 July when Youbi received a four months' suspended sentence and three years' suspension of civic rights. Madaci was jailed for two years (but the sentence reflected other crimes). The defence was heavily criticised for suggesting that the police had lied.

## 4. O.....B..... (defence counsel)

This case involved a young black woman who worked in a chemist's shop. Her boss was trying to get rid of her. It was not made clear why he wanted to dismiss his employee but we may assume from what happened that he thought she had cheated him and, in particular, that she had stolen money. He employed someone to trap the woman, who was then accused of short-changing the man of an absurdly small amount of money. This was the reason then given for her dismissal.

Advised by her lawyer, she sued her boss for unfair dismissal and won her case.

What clinched the case was the fact that the supposedly anonymous customer could refer to the young woman as a Camerounaise. This implied that he had been given details about her, since the barrister, herself a black woman, pointed out that she would be quite unable to tell where a black person came from.

## 5. January 1995 incident

On a cold January night a young man of Tunisian origin wearing a hooded *blouson* was attacked by the police in the alleyway of his parents' flat. The young man says that soon after he left home he realised that he had forgotten his cigarettes. He ran back and as he was climbing the stairs to his parents' flat three policemen followed him. When they tried to stop him a scuffle broke out alerting the rest of the family and neighbours. The young man's father and his younger brother who came to the rescue were allegedly extremely roughly treated by the police and all three men ended up at the police station with a number of bruises.

SOS Racisme and their lawyer started court proceedings against the police and the case is continuing.

### 6. Mourad Tchier, 27 December 1993

*Educateurs de prévention* is the name given to people who work closely with young people on an estate. The service itself is called the Service de Prévention et de Sauvegarde de l'Adolescence du Rhône. This type of education is not supported by the local or national education authorities but by the social services. It has its own budget and provides teachers and social workers who are associated entirely with one area and act as the first port of call in emergencies. This is the closest I could find to a victim support system.

I interviewed an *éducatrice de prévention*, a young woman who worked on the estate (Bron Parilly) where Mourad Tchier lived. The youth was shot by the police on 27 December 1993. The incident happened in the following way. Four young men were travelling in a stolen car which two officers in a police car recognised and chased. This took the youths and the policemen into a cul de sac where the youths abandoned the car and tried to climb up a fairly steep bank. Three youths were wearing dark *blousons*, a fourth one, Mourad Tchier, wore a yellow *blouson*. One policeman (in his fifties) chased them. He was armed and shot the more visible youth dead. Another youth fell and was injured, but was not shot at. This happened in the late evening.

When Mourad did not appear the following day his friends started agitating and found out what had happened to him. When they discovered that his body was in the morgue they informed the *éducatrice* immediately. She contacted the police, who said that they would call on Mourad's mother and inform her of what had happened. But when the *éducatrice* called on Mourad's mother later that day, she found that the police had not been in touch with her, and it was therefore she who had to tell the mother what had happened to her son. She then took the mother to the morgue. A few months later, when the mother decided that her son should be buried in Algeria, it was again the *éducatrice* who accompanied her and the coffin to the plane.

Mourad was a gifted young man, a 'tagger' (a street artist) who had received some official recognition, and a student with very good educational qualifications. The onus was on the *éducatrice* to defuse a very hostile situation, since all the youths of the estate and their friends outside were outraged by the killing. The anger and energy released were channelled through a number of initiatives: a magazine, an exhibition of Mourad's work, and a big football match. The *éducatrice*, the only person who does not have an immigrant background in an immigrant community where 53 nationalities have been officially recorded, orchestrated these activities.

A defence counsel initiated a court case, yet by March 1995 it had not yet come to a hearing. The policeman in question was still in the same post he had occupied in 1983, and was still allowed to carry a weapon.

The facts were that a car was stolen and that it contained four youths, one black and three of Maghrébin origin. Whether or not the police response was racially motivated, it tells us a great deal about police practice and culture in France. Amnesty International, in its report on France, considered the case of Mourad Tchier and concluded first, that policemen in France are trained to shoot to kill and, secondly, that the policemen's reaction was disproportionate to the seriousness of the crime.

The family was treated very badly indeed. When the police were asked directly by the *éducatrice* why they had not visited Mourad's mother to inform her of his death, their explanations were quite lame and unacceptable: they thought she had been visited by police officers from another division. There seemed to be no possibility of a court hearing providing her with the comfort of seeing justice done, since no trial had taken place almost two years after the event.

The opinion of the defence counsel is that:

> ... to put it charitably, one might say that the courts are overworked and over-stretched, or less charitably and perhaps more realistically, that they are totally at a loss since the *juge d'instruction* has to rely so heavily on the police for his investigation.

This point is often made not only by defence counsel but also by judges themselves. The court in the French system depends on the cooperation of the police for its investigation and it therefore becomes very difficult to find fault with police behaviour, 'since we have to rely on their evidence', as one judge said.

## 7. Expulsion of Tziganes from Romania

This case involved people from Romania who entered France and ended up in Lyons, no one really knows how, but certainly illegally. They were left to fend for themselves, literally, on the street one Saturday, and were moved on without being given the chance or the time to seek asylum in France. Thirteen families were eventually broken up: the men were sent to a detention centre, the women to a Salvation Army hostel, and some of the children were actually separated from their parents.

The association Tiberius Claudius took up their case and fought it on the question of timing. At a time when all the offices of the Préfecture were closed and when it was impossible for the new arrivals to obtain and fill in the various application forms for asylum, the police worked extremely fast to interview everyone, record their declarations and notify the asylum seekers that they would be taken back to the frontier. The point made by the association (through its two barristers) was that such a procedure was in contravention of French regulations on asylum and the Geneva Convention. The case was heard at the court of the Tribunal Administratif. It was a public hearing in the presence of the press and local television. The judge gave his decision on the following day: he upheld the decision of the Prefect to refuse entry and to return the Romanian families to the frontier. The two barristers contested the decision and were considering an appeal to the Conseil d'Etat. However, soon after the court's decision, a chartered plane arrived with asylum seekers from Paris to pick up the Romanians in Lyons and take them all back to Romania.

The case of the expulsion of the Romanian families highlights the conflict between the administration and the judiciary on questions of asylum and nationality. As Judge Seyz put it in an interview on 1 November 1994, 'the decision of the Prefect is always upheld in cases of repatriation'. This does not bode well at all, since the police know that their actions are unlikely to be challenged in the present climate of public opinion in France.

The Procureur Général was asked to adjudicate on the question of handcuffs, which surfaced in the case of the asylum seekers from Romania. All the men had been transferred from the detention centre in Sainte Foye (a suburb of Lyons) and taken to the Tribunal Administratif in handcuffs (hands behind their back), with each pair of handcuffs linked by a chain to a police officer. When the hearing was due to start, in a very small room, each Romanian accompanied by his attendant policeman had to squeeze in, as well as the women and children (all in tears – this was the first time they had been reunited since the previous Saturday), the journalists, the representative of the Préfecture, two barristers, the President of the Tribunal Administratif and his attendant, and any one who wished to attend since the hearing was public. The President, Monsieur Fontanelle, decided to ask the police officers to uncuff the men and to leave the court room, allowing only two of them to guard the door.

According to the press, the Procureur Général did not condone or condemn the action of the police, he simply quoted the official text and let it be known that the decision of the police in these matters was final; it was for them to decide whether an individual might run away or be violent. In the case of asylum seekers, in tears and unable to understand a word of French or actually know what was happening to them without the help of an interpreter, the use of handcuffs seemed somewhat overcautious.

In September 1995 the question of the handcuffs had not been resolved, and foreigners, asylum seekers and illegal immigrants continued to arrive in court handcuffed and shackled to police officers with chains.

## 8. Marriage and the threat of nationality laws

Marriages of convenience have come under the spotlight in many European countries. The authorities in France can now issue an 'opposition' to a marriage, which can only be fought through the courts.

A young Angolan man who had studied in France and was officially an asylum seeker when he decided to marry his French girl friend, received an 'opposition' to his marriage. Only after a court case and the decision of the Tribunal de Grande Instance in Lyons to annul the interdiction issued by the Procureur were they able to get married.

On 1 February 1995 the Cour de Cassation (Supreme Court of Appeal) decided that a foreigner who had committed a crime could be expelled from France after serving his sentence, according to the provisions of a law passed after he was convicted. This amounted to a retrospective penalty. The decision rested on the division between the penal and the police/administrative systems, and the Cour de Cassation decided that the expulsion decree should be considered merely as a police measure.

The case itself can be summed up as follows: Hassen Hamoudi, a 33-year old Algerian born in France, was condemned to 14 years in prison for murder in 1984. There was no question then of his expulsion from France, thanks to the Loi sur les Etrangers (Foreigners Law). Four years later, however, he was sentenced to expulsion and this was justified under the 1986 Pasqua law. Hamoudi refused to board the plane due to take him to Algeria, which was a foreign country for him, and he was given an additional two months in prison. His barristers (working for Groupe d'Information et de Soutien aux Travailleurs Immigrés (GISTI)) requested a review of his case.

The decision by the Cour de Cassation overturned what was understood to be law until 1991, namely that the principle that laws cannot be retrospective applied equally to immigration, until the following judgement was passed:

> The expulsion of foreigners is not a penalty but a preventive measure taken by the police, aimed exclusively at protecting public order and security, and it may therefore be applied to sentences which precede the promulgation of the law on which it is based.

This decision has a wider application, since the second Pasqua law on foreigners in 1993, like the 1986 law, took away some protection from foreigners even if they had lived in France since childhood. The foreign parents of French children and the foreign husband or wife of French nationals can now be expelled from France if they have been sentenced to prison for more than five years. Moreover, the decision can now be retrospective.

## THE PASQUA EFFECT[14]

For the police, the Pasqua effect resulted in 'quieter suburbs'. In their view, stopping people and asking them to prove their identity was admissible because surveillance was necessary to eradicate illegal immigration.

In his interview, Father Delorme expressed the hope that the Pasqua effect may serve to restrain 'les bavures de la police'. He was mainly referring to those cases well known in France, and also documented by Amnesty International, where the police were themselves guilty of criminal behaviour (racial or other). He felt that the Minister, as a strong advocate of law and order, although supportive of the police, would want to watch over them.

---

14. On the Pasqua laws, see pp 23-4.

CRARDA and SOS Racisme thought that the Pasqua effect was dangerous, since it did not offer a solution to the real problems of poverty, drugs and crime but contributed to the destabilisation of a whole group of people who did not have the backing of the indigenous population and had not yet managed to organise themselves in a strong community – in fact, the opposite was the case, since the old network of family, *quartiers* (districts), workplace, and unions had all but come apart, leaving the individual much more vulnerable.

By September 1995 Pasqua was no longer a Minister, but the legislation he had introduced was still in place. A new government and its Interior Minister, Jean Louis Debré, had not softened the policy towards foreigners or asylum seekers. France had experienced a wave of terrorism starting in August 1995 with a bomb in the Paris métro. This continued with the discovery of a bomb on the TGV railway line north of Lyons and the bombing of a Jewish school in Villeurbanne at the beginning of September.

The main suspect of the attempted destruction of the railway line, Khaled Kelkal, aged 24, lived in Vaulx en Velin. He was only just an Algerian citizen, since he came to France at the age of one month. Khaled escaped when the police raided his camp on a hillside in Vaugneray and wounded Karim Koussa, one of three men who had come to bring him food. Police investigators said that the fingerprints on the device on the railway line were those of Khaled and also that one of the shotguns found by Khaled's sleeping bag was the one used in the assassination in July of a Paris Imam, Abdelbaki Sahraoui, a co-founder of Algeria's FIS (Islamic Salvation Front). It was not suggested that Khaled was the gunman.

Khaled was shot on the night of Friday 29 September after police paratroopers allegedly returned fire. The shooting sparked a riot in the Lyons suburb where he and his family lived, and youths were said to be responsible for setting cars on fire. There were other sporadic eruptions of violence later that month.

## THE POLICE

### The police and public relations

This section is based on interviews carried out at the Hôtel de Police in Lyons in the autumn of 1994. The officer responsible for contact between the police and the public accentuated the positive steps taken by the force, for example giving talks to schools and making contact with representatives of the various communities. The police welcomed the opening of a mosque because they felt that the emergence of recognised leaders of the Muslim communities would facilitate dialogue between the various authorities, along the lines established by the Jewish community. Communication between the police and the local community was considered vital to greater integration of minority groups in French society. Efforts were also being made to make the police entrance examination more accessible to French people of Maghrébin, West Indian or Vietnamese origin.

The police considered France to be a generous country which opened its doors to everyone, and said that it was enormously difficult to send anyone back to their country of origin. In their view, the main threat of violence came from newly arrived groups of Poles, who were described as being particularly prone to fighting and using guns and other weapons. The police saw the suburbs as being fairly quiet at that time, with most attacks committed by a delinquent, mafioso group, and they were coping well with that.

The police public relations officer did not think there was any discrimination in the allocation of accommodation, and mentioned that FNAIM and CPI, both state controlled property companies, had never been cited for their discriminatory policies.

Poles are the most recent ethnic minority group in Lyons, preceded by Turks and, because of France's involvement in Indo China, the Vietnamese. Each of these groups was seen as fairly self-contained, in particular the Vietnamese; they had recognisable occupations or were employed in well defined sectors. They had come as single people and were soon followed by their families. The small village of Saint Maurice de Beynost, which received a large number of Vietnamese at the time of the boat exodus, was cited as an example of seamless integration. Blacks from the West Indies (Antillais), who work mainly in hospitals, were considered, on the whole, to be well established members of the Lyons community. African Blacks, who came to France more recently, were, the police said, often the butt of attacks by other groups such as the Turks. In this rapid classification the Maghrébins were not mentioned at all. The various groups of immigrants were seen as cohesive even if, like the Poles, they did fight among themselves.

## Interviews with senior officers

The policing of large events and demonstrations falls within the remit of a special section at the Hôtel de Police. It is responsible for a large part of Lyons and the surrounding area: nine *arrondissements*, 13 *communes* and Villefranche, Givors and Tarrare, which are bigger than *communes* and some distance from Lyons. At the time of the research, the section was busy organising policing operations for the opening of the mosque, although (rightly as it turned out) they did not expect any trouble.

The police records for the preceding weekend, 23–26 September, did not include reports of any racially motivated offences. However, the reports did not give any details about the ethnic groups of either the accused or the victim and, occasionally, no identity was mentioned at all.

In contrast with the optimistic picture offered by the public relations section, some senior officers were very frank about the state of the force. It was, they said, '... an ageing force quite unable to attract young recruits and in particular recruits coming from ethnic minority groups'. The Ecole Nationale de la Police is in Saint Cyr au Mont D'Or, a small town very near Lyons, and this view was quite reliable. Senior officers also deplored the conditions in which immigrant workers and their families were housed: they had witnessed, in the late 1950s and early 1960s (during and after the Algerian War of Independence), the increasing concentration of families in unsuitable accommodation, and concluded that 'what was supposed to be a temporary solution became a permanent one'.

On crime and minorities, the police were sceptical about the national figures published by INSEE – the Lyons force was never asked to produce such statistics for its own area. According to a senior officer, 'one person out of nine is going to be the victim of a crime' in France. Furthermore, INSEE figures show that 32 per cent of convictions are for crimes committed by foreigners, but if the crime of irregular entry into the country is subtracted, the figure falls to 20 per cent. The senior officers thought that, although the police were vigilant and had successfully 'accompanied clandestine immigrants' to the frontier, it was probably also the case that people simply vanished into France.

In September 1994 the Lyons police gave the following figures for expulsions in 1993:

- 450 *mandats de dépot*

- 556 *reconduits à la frontière*

- 31 expulsions

- 587 people were requested to leave, and 413 left.

The failure of the Lyons police to send back Youbi and Madaci, the two young Maghrébin men who were found guilty of throwing stones at the police during the demonstration of March 1993, was summed up in the following words:

> ... they were two young men born in France of Maghrébin parents. They had not yet applied for French nationality. They were both deported, but they both returned to France.

The police saw racial crime as anti-semitic attacks against individual property (for example graffiti) and synagogues, and the desecration of Jewish cemeteries. Three such incidents were mentioned in police records for 1994, and three in 1993. A senior police officer said that he thought:

> ... the mafioso aspect of the Maghrébin community was growing, and that three-quarters of crimes committed were committed by people of Maghrébin origin.

He insisted that the family unit was crumbling in such communities, with fathers preferring to return to the Maghreb rather than see their role and authority completely denied by their children. The mothers who stayed behind were often duped by their children, but they were loyal to them as well as dependent on them for money.

The attacks against a young Maghrébin in a train  – three soldiers pushed him out of a moving train – and a youth killed by a bouncer, were, according to the police, barbarous acts that are dealt with as such by the courts and severely punished.

During the period of the research, police activities in Lyons intensified in two areas: the fight against illegal immigration, and the search for suspected terrorists after an explosive device was found on the railway track of the TGV north of Lyons.

## POLITICAL PARTIES AND RACIALLY MOTIVATED CRIME

At the 1993 parliamentary elections, the association France Plus supported candidates from ethnic minorities in the suburbs of Lyons. Anxious to establish its independence from established parties like the Greens, the Communist Party or the Socialist Party, its campaign slogan was *on roule pour nous* (we run for ourselves).[15] The results were disappointing and did not improve much at the 1995 municipal elections. This tendency towards 'political auto-organisation', based not on religious distinctions but citizenship, is counterbalanced by the associations of young Muslims. At the end of 1993 a congress of Young Muslims was attended by 1,200 young people (many coming from as far afield as Paris).

In autumn 1994 when work on this project started, and when a rather dull presidential campaign was getting under way, the message from the extreme right had lost some of its stridency: Charles Pasqua's laws on nationality, repatriation, illegal immigration and expulsion had more or less met the demands of Le Pen and his Front National (FN) supporters. The police did not even consider the presence in Lyons of Bruno Golnisch (Professor of Japanese at Lyon II), the FN's number two man, as a problem. Father Delorme, however, insisted that political discourse had been slow to change and to condemn racist and xenophobic language and behaviour in France.

The police position was that if all was quiet in the *banlieues* there was no problem. But the force was an ageing one, in which the largest group still was the *pieds noirs*, French settlers in Algeria and their descendants, who had returned to France in angry mood, believing that the French government had abandoned them after they had suffered attacks by the FLN (Front de Libération Nationale) and lost their status and possessions. They continued to treat Maghrébins in France as they had treated them in Algeria. Since the *pieds noirs* spoke some Arabic, it had been assumed by the authorities that they would be suitable for the job of controlling a troublesome Maghrébin population.

In spring 1995 France chose Jacques Chirac as the new president to replace the retiring Socialist, François Mitterand. The local elections were held six weeks later and, like the presidential elections, took place in two ballots, with continuous campaigning from March until 17 June. On the whole, people showed much more interest in the local elections. They did not favour the candidates in the Chirac camp, and the FN did as well as had

---

15. On the sides and backs of large lorries one can read 'je roule pour vous' which can be loosely translated as 'I run for you'. The candidates adapted this, saying 'We run for ourselves'.

been predicted, with the party taking a number of towns from the Communist Party. The Socialist Party more or less maintained its position. In the elections for the senate in September, notwithstanding Le Pen's claims of a complete victory, his party did not gain a single seat.

During the presidential campaign, a group of four FN members were fly-posting at night in Marseilles when one of them shot and killed a young Frenchman of Comorean origin. Le Pen was of the view that if the FN members had not been armed they would have been killed,[17] while Balladur and Chirac, both presidential candidates holding high office in government at the time, condemned the action but did not take the opportunity to issue a positive statement. This may explain the decision by five organisations in Lyons – Agir Ensemble pour les Droits de l'Homme, LICRA, Ligue des Droits de l'Homme, MRAP, and SOS Racisme – to launch a campaign of vigilance by calling a press conference on Wednesday 15 March. They announced the creation of a Comité de Vigilance contre le Racisme et la Xénophobie et pour le Bon Déroulement de la Campagne Electorale (Watch Committee against Racism and Xenophobia and for the Proper Conduct of the Election Campaign).

The main thrust of the campaign was to condemn the action of the FN member, to monitor everyday incidents of racism, to campaign against the Pasqua laws which had created difficulties for many people – mixed couples, foreign parents of French children who could not be deported but could not be granted legal right of abode[16] – and to reaffirm the *droit du sol* (citizenship by birth on French territory). The organisations also pledged to monitor the election campaigns of the candidates and to initiate legal actions in cases of racism and xenophobia.

All this amounted to a considerable commitment for the associations, which were staffed largely by volunteers who who had other jobs (except for the vice president of LICRA, who had retired). As *partie civile*, they were investing a lot of time and money on trust, since the process is expensive. They also had to rely on information passed on to them, as they could not be expected to attend every meeting during the election.

At the same press conference, it was also announced that the trade union CGT and SOS Racisme had called meetings on the issues raised by the Pasqua law. Anti-semitic and anti-Arab pamphlets, allegedly the work of the FN, and not new to activists in ethnic minority organisations, were also rather reluctantly passed around.

In June 1995 the Comité de Vigilance had no case of 'misbehaviour' to report during the election campaign. The killing of the young Comorean in Marseilles, which had galvanised the associations into action during the presidential campaign, did not inspire the same vigilance during the municipal elections where the results were much more likely to be biased towards the extreme right – Jean Marie Le Pen and his party had fielded 25,000 FN candidates. The FN were hugely successful in the first round of the elections

---

16. On this last point both legislation and police action are moving very fast. On 12 April 1995 I learned of a case where the Algerian mother of a child of ten, born in France, was given two weeks to leave the country.

17. *Le Nouvel Observateur*, 22 February 1996.

and, although the final result was less dramatic, many town halls now have FN members and a few are headed by an FN mayor or sympathiser.

The local elections raised the possibility of campaigning for or against an anti-immigration platform. However, apart from demands expressed by the extreme right, such as the withdrawal of all national support to associations helping foreigners or immigrants and the withdrawal of social housing to the same categories of people, it is interesting to note that the nationality laws introduced more recently by Pasqua did not come in for criticism, although many French people are now realising that these laws may very well affect their own lives even if they are not immigrants themselves.

In order to renew their identity cards, French people – whatever their age – must now, under the new law, produce the date and place of birth of their parents. A retired French school teacher, for example, suddenly found that her French parents who had lived in Algeria were now reclassified as *pieds noirs,* and that she herself, who was born in France of French parents, was similarly classified, which she strongly rejected. Since the regulations were still fairly new, the outcry during the period of my enquiry was limited to letters to newspapers and the odd press article.

A pamphlet issued by the FN candidate in Saint Fons (a Lyons suburb with a predominantly Maghrébin population) mentioned as its first item the necessity to return Saint Fons to the French and rid it of all foreigners. It also made strong accusations of corruption against the existing candidate, a member of the Socialist Party. Such extreme attacks are hardly counterbalanced by the efforts of individuals of Maghrébin origin who put themselves forward for election.

At least two of the associations in Lyons have members actively committed to taking part in the political life of the city – Djida Tadzait (JALB), who had lost her seat at the European Parliament, was trying to find an electoral list which would accept her for the municipal elections of June 1995. In September it was confirmed that she did not succeed. Agora presented a list of candidates and polled seven per cent of the votes in an area not renowned for its active participation in local elections. Both the initiative and the result were claimed as a victory.

## RACIAL HARASSMENT AND DISCRIMINATION IN HOUSING AND EDUCATION

### Housing

High concentrations of immigrant families are found in French suburbs, according to a report in 1995 by the National Institute for Demographic Studies (INED). There are also pockets of settlement in older properties in city centres. Whereas European immigrants settle in areas which do not have a high proportion of immigrants, new migrants from Turkey, Algeria, Morocco and Asia tend to live in immigrant areas. The result, INED concludes, is a form of ghettoisation leading to segregation. These findings are confirmed in Lyons by the Mission Régionale d'Information sur l'Exclusion[18] (MRIE or Regional Mission for Information on Exclusion).

The following sections are based on a long interview with Monsieur Gachet, the Director of Action Lyonnaise pour l'Insertion Sociale par le Logement (ALPIL), on documents from SIAL (Service Inter Administratif du Logement) which is housed at the Lyons Préfecture, and on a study published in November 1994 by the MRIE entitled *Faire progresser le droit d'habiter en Rhône Alpes*.

## MRIE

The director of MRIE, Monsieur Alberto Lopez, gave me the latest INSEE figures on housing for the most disadvantaged people in the Lyons area, and also spoke very frankly about the difficulties he encountered when he presented the results of his latest study, *Conditions de logement dans l'agglomération Lyonnaise*, to the local authorities.

In the latest edition of the MRIE bulletin (March 1995) the only reasons given for people having to leave their accommodation were debts or the fact that the landlord wanted the flat back. There was no mention of cases of aggressive behaviour by neighbours, and I was told that the police would only get involved if there were *coups et blessures* (bodily harm). The director of MRIE, who is on the administrative council of an HLM unit, said that he had never had a case of racially motivated crime.

Racial discrimination, rather than racially motivated crime, was the term used to describe the circumstances in which people who were initially housed in *centres d'hébergement* or *foyers*[19] found themselves. These centres are often concentrated in a particular area of the city, and the local authorities refuse (or are reluctant) to house or rehouse all accommodation seekers. Because there is very little flexibility and cooperation between the various councils, the last hope of people living in what was originally meant to be temporary accommodation is to appeal to SIAL.

In the section of MRIE's report on housing allocation, 'the foreign origin – real or supposed' of the person requesting accommodation is said to be 'one of the factors influencing the decision of the services of the SIAL'. One of the reasons that SIAL itself gives for the non-allocation of housing is the fact that an applicant may not be recognised as a resident of the *commune* or district. Moreover, if applicants come from a *centre d'hébergement* or a *foyer* they will definitely not qualify. The other two reasons are lack of resources and the 'social balance' of a residential block or area.

---

18. Exclusion is also known as *la grande pauvreté* (extreme poverty).

19. These centres and foyers are temporary accommodation, either bed and breakfast or buildings such as *Les sans abris*, for example, run by the Catholic church in partnership with the district authorities; or the foyers SONACOTRA, which originally gave accommodation to single immigrant workmen but are now more often the first accommodation refugee families will know. See also section on CRARDA, p 75.

## SIAL

The Service Inter Administratif du Logement (SIAL) is relatively recent. It was created in 1992 specifically to meet the needs of the most disadvantaged people seeking accommodation or looking for better accommodation. It has the support and the cooperation of the Préfecture, the Direction Départementale de l'Equipement (DDE) and the Direction Départementale des Affairs Sanitaires et Sociales (DDAS). This multi-agency initiative at the level of the *département* replaced, but also learned from, the previous Bureau du Logement de la Préfecture.

In November 1994 SIAL published *Evolution de la demande prioritaire de logement enregistrée au SIAL en 1994* (Evolution of emergency requests for housing registered by SIAL in 1994). The first sentence of the report reads:

> On the 30th of November 1994, SIAL had registered 7,005 requests for housing, of which 59 per cent were from French nationals.

The nationality of the other applicants was not mentioned at this point. SIAL's intention was either to stress the pauperisation of the French population or to forestall the often heard criticism that foreigners are better treated than French nationals. SIAL also published a series of tables giving details of the 6,241 applications they dealt with between December 1993 and November 1994, including a table on the nationality of the applicants. French nationals accounted for the largest number, followed by Algerians, 'Others', and then Tunisians, Moroccans and people from the EC. The graph grouped Algerians, Tunisians and Moroccans together under the heading of Maghreb.

The report reveals the extent of the housing shortage when it states that in 1993 SIAL could satisfy 1,569 housing or re-housing requests, and in 1994 1,874 requests, whereas the number of applications ran at over 6,000. The shortage is more easily estimated in the area of social housing (such as HLM), but the private sector does not provide enough accommodation to mop up the shortfall. The poorest people are often housed in the precarious private sector, either in very cheap accommodation or as part of an extended family or in multi-occupation.

It is impossible to study the occurrence of racially motivated crime in such a context, since the agencies function only as suppliers of accommodation, and consider non-payment of rent as the only reason for expulsion. They do not intervene for any other reason, and see racially motivated crime as a police matter.

## ALPIL

ALPIL was created in 1979 to respond to the housing problems of foreigners and low income families who were the victims of poor housing in the city. Lyons had embarked on a programme of rejuvenation and slum clearance which left the poorer inhabitants very vulnerable. If poor housing was the problem of the 1970s, the problem of the 1990s is no housing or at least no permanent accommodation, and what ALPIL calls 'illegal housing and illegitimate people'.

When I visited the ALPIL offices, which are situated in the old silk weaving district of Lyons next to one of the main squares of the city, with a high concentration of Maghrébin and Turkish shopkeepers, a Tzigane woman and three children had been brought along by a police officer because she was begging in the street. She did not speak French and the gendarme had guessed, correctly, that she had no address.

In 1993 1,000 families went through ALPIL's reception services. Applicants included those who did not find accommodation through other channels, as well as those who did have accommodation but were in difficulties because they could not pay or because they had to meet the demands of unreasonable landlords or face eviction. ALPIL's aim is to empower the tenant, and it offers help when necessary, and particularly if a court case is likely. ALPIL has a lawyer who specialises in housing problems, and it also acts as *partie civile* and initiates legal actions.

None of the court cases mentioned in the interview and in answer to my direct question were said to be of a racial nature. ALPIL can call on the help of social workers, family groups and district associations which intervene in neighbourhood feuds, but the examples mentioned involved the behaviour of children, noise and smells.

In partnership with other authorities, ALPIL works on projects aimed at increasing the supply of housing units. It also has contact with housing agents and agencies. Most of ALPIL's initiatives are the result of multi-agency efforts, and it was felt by Monsieur Gachet that this was really the best solution. The Besson Law of 1990 provided the impetus (and funding) for regional initiatives, and spurred on the association's housing projects and initiatives. ALPIL initiated the rehabilitation of a number of rooming houses in the inner city, and continues to do so.

It is obvious that a large number of the cases going through ALPIL come from racial minorities. When asked, for example, if ALPIL used a quota system for social housing units, the director said 'No' and laughed, adding as a joke that, previously:

> ... suburbs with a large proportion of social housing had a 10 per cent quota. This was broken down as 10 per cent of foreigners, 5 per cent of which were Algerians.

## Education

Some problems have been mentioned already: school places are refused to minority members, and the special educational needs of the poorest children are not met, as in Saint Jean. I was not told of any examples of racial violence within or around schools, but did learn from the director of the MRIE that there had been recent cases of racial harassment against a small number of Pakistani families and especially against their children, who had had to be sent to fee-paying schools in order to avoid problems.

# RECOMMENDATIONS AND CONCLUSIONS

## Recommendations

*Legal advice*

In a system where the law and legal procedure are so important, the main demand from associations dealing with the problems of people from ethnic minorities was for the financing of specialist barristers. At the moment these associations rely on young barristers at the beginning of their careers who have to move on when they can no longer survive on the 900 F that each of these cases brings. This means that their expertise is lost and that new barristers have to be found and briefed.

*Victim support*

A number of organisations offer support to the victims of racial crime, but it was felt that this was often on an *ad hoc* basis, and that a high profile organisation would be beneficial, particularly in cases of blatant discrimination. Such an organisation could also shield the witnesses in cases of attack or discrimination.

*Housing*

There is an ambivalent attitude towards collecting information on the allocation of housing (especially in social housing units such as HLM). A register of tenants according to well defined criteria could defuse accusations of discrimination.

## Conclusions

It is worth restating here that racially motivated crime is not a French concept: racism and xenophobia are the terms that are most widely used in France.

Asked how things could be improved or radically changed, none of the people interviewed suggested the introduction of measures to record the racial content of crime. Most criticism was levelled at the working of the courts and at the weight of the police role in the judicial system. The diminishing powers of the judiciary in the face of the growing powers of the administrative legislation delivered by the Préfecture was also deplored.

If France is inactive about the recognition of racially motivated crime it is unfortunately well ahead on the development of regulations and measures to discourage immigration, legal or illegal, with all the consequences that implies for an often vulnerable population.

That racism and xenophobia exist in France is not in doubt, nor that there is a genuine effort to combat it, especially on the part of the judiciary. The waters are muddied when it comes to the question of nationality and right of abode. We witness, on the part of the authorities responsible for the administration of such regulations, a certain overenthusiasm, mainly in the frequent demands for proof of identity from anyone (but usually young men) with an easily recognisable profile.

France is still trying to cope with the legacy of its colonial past and, to a certain extent, with its immigration policies. It is trying to solve the problems through the bias of nationality laws. It is evident that these laws, with the constant threat they represent to many families, have a destabilising effect on individuals and groups who are already in difficulty because of the present economic situation.

France and the French authorities seem to be unaware of (or at least refuse to acknowledge) the failure of a strong republican integrationist policy. The writer Azouz Begag, himself a success story in French terms, is a lone voice who, in his book *Quartiers Sensibles* (co-authored with Father Delorme), raises the spectre of the failure of the French model of integration, particularly its insistence on the importance of the integration of the individual and its unwillingness to recognise allegiance to another group.

Begag sees the rise of Islam and its activities in the *banlieues* as a direct result of such a failure, particularly in areas where national and local authorities are considered to have failed. For young people in the *banlieues* without work and without hope – the same people whom Segaud of the Saint Jean Centre d'Animation referred to as the 'lost generation' – Islam offers personal salvation rather than solidarity with the family group. In the words of one interviewee:

> If you are good and do good works you will discover a light within yourself, you will be at peace with yourself.

It is also the promise for the young of a brotherhood, but a very exclusive brotherhood, which, for example, rejects the older generation and, of course, women.

In *Arabicides*, Fausto Giudice gives an account of the violent deaths of more than 300 people from minorities in France. The (mis)behaviour of the police, too, is well documented, in reports such as Amnesty International's. The police themselves are making substantial efforts, but they only see the *quartiers difficiles* in terms of delinquency. The legislation of January 1995 makes a number of recommendations including: more policemen on the beat; *ilotage*, (a form of community policing); more regular police contact with small areas; and the right of the police to enter communal parts of housing estates.

The hatred that young people in the *quartiers* have for the police (*les keufs*) is tenacious. The big word in the suburbs now is *la haine* (hatred), and a recent film documents the phenomenon. This hatred is individualised and finds its expression in the purchase of fire arms or drug dealing and drug abuse. It is aimed at the police, but also at those from 'outside', who do not live on the deprived housing estates, and at anyone in authority.

Jean Costil, director of CIMADE, very wisely recommended that we should not be tempted to make the authorities the worst culprits. His argument was:

> ... that they are big, they are more visible and therefore their behaviour is for us all to see, we can condemn them and this makes us feel good but we have to beware – there is worse.

Whereas some people see the values of citizenship as the salvation of a sick society and want to give school children lessons in civic education, for many it is too late and republican values amount to very little if you are unemployed and likely to lose (or have already lost) your accommodation as well.

There are provisions in the French criminal code that prohibit seven kinds of racist crime, including two forms of discrimination as well as racist attacks and insults. However, these provisions are little used. There are a number of possible reasons. First, there is no specific enforcement mechanism. Secondly, complainants do not have direct access to the courts; they have to act through the police and in most cases are reluctant to do so (this applies to racial discrimination as well as racial attacks). Thirdly, as mentioned by the judge of the Lyons Tribunal and the associations, there are few advocates with experience of handling cases brought under these provisions. Fourthly, there are inherent difficulties in gathering evidence which are not addressed in the existing enforcement arrangements. Finally, most victims lack the financial resources needed to pursue a case.

The special provisions continue to be of little use, in spite of the efforts of the Ministry of Justice to publicise them and to encourage members of the legal professions to make use of them. The most common attitude among the police and the legal professions is that:

> ... a crime is a crime and should be punished as such, the motive, whether racist or other is irrelevant.

However, advocates in particular point out that the punishment of the offender, in cases where the racial motive is evident and well documented, is out of proportion to the injury suffered by the victim.

The intense and wide-ranging crackdown on illegal immigration is officially presented as an attack only on those who do not have residence rights. In practice, however, police sweeps are directed at members of minority groups in general, so that the official policy stigmatises whole communities, and particularly those originating from the Maghreb. At the same time, the specific provisions against racist crime rely on the police for their enforcement. This can hardly work when the police also have responsibility for the drive against illegal immigrants which stigmatises minority communities as a whole. Furthermore, certain racist acts by the police have become notorious.

Duval Smith in a recent article in *The Guardian* stated (without giving his source) that one in four people in France has a grandmother who was not born in France. This suggests two lines of thought: on the one hand, that France has been rather successful in its integration policy, and on the other, that the 'recent nationals' are also the most ardent zealots.

# REFERENCES

Amnesty International, *France Coups de Feu, Homicides et Allégations de Mauvais Traitements de la Part d'Agents de la Force Publique*, 12 October 1994. This report contains among other cases that of Mourad Tchier documented in the section on court cases.

Begag, A and C Delorme, *Quartiers sensibles*, Point Virgule, Editions du Seuil, 1994.

Bjorgo, Tore and Rob Whitte (eds), *Racist Violence in Europe*, MacMillan, London, 1993.

Commission consultative des Droits de l'Homme, *Racially Motivated Crime in France, Statistics for 1991 and 1992*. Report.

Forbes, I and G Mead, *Measure for Measure*, Equal Opportunities Studies Group, University of Southampton, 1992.

Gerholm, Tomas and Yngve Georg Lithman (eds), *The New Islamic Presence in Western Europe*, Mansell, London, 1998.

INED, *Le Logement des Immigrés*, Paris, July, 1995.

INSEE, on housing.

Jazouli, A, *Une Saison en Banlieu*, Plon, Paris, 1995.

La documentation française, *La Lutte contre le Racisme et la Xénophobie*, 1990.

La documentation française, *Aspects de la Criminalité et de la Délinquance constatées en France en 1993 par les Services de Police et de Gendarmerie d'après les Statistiques de la Police Judiciaire*, Paris, 1993.

Laferrière, F J, 'Frontières du droit Frontières des Droits', in *Préface*, L'Harmattan/ANAFE, Paris, 1993.

Ministre de la Justice, *Guide des Lois Antiracistes*, September, 1994.

MRIE on housing in the Lyons Area.

Perrin-Martin, J P, *Amalgames*, L'Harmattan, Paris, 1994.

Tournier, P and Robert, P, *Etrangers et Délinquances*, L'Harmattan, Paris, 1991.

Vidal, *Code Civil*, Paris, new edition, September, 1994.

Villeurbanne, Site Saint Jean, Betsam Essassi, Banlieuescopies, December, 1994.

Weil, P, *La France et ses Etrangers*, Gallimard, Paris, 1992.

Press coverage for the Lyons area (and from further afield) for the duration of the project on the attacks against people from ethnic minorities, extracts mainly from the local paper *Le Progrès* and the two national papers *Le Monde* and *Libération*. During the life of the project *Libération* lost its Lyons bureau but kept some reporters, such as Bernard Fromentin, in the city.

# CHAPTER FOUR

# ROME

## Jolanda Chirico

## INTRODUCTION

Italians have been discovering their own racism in a manner peculiar to this Latin, Catholic country. While Italy has had a long experience of migration, both within and from outside the country, it is only in recent years that increasing numbers of migrants from outside Europe have settled. Racism was brought on to the public agenda in 1989 by the murder of Jerry Maslo, the desecration of Jewish religious places of worship and a general escalation of racially motivated incidents across Italy. For example:

- February 1990. Some 200 people, masked and armed with baseball bats and iron bars, organised the beating of blacks and Gypsies in the town centre of Florence on the night of the Carnival, wounding a number of them.

- March 1990. The violence spread to Rome, Varese, Turin, Caserta, Catania, Livorno, Matera, Milan, etc. There were Molotov cocktail attacks on immigrants and evictions from rented accommodation.

- In Rome, a fire bomb was thrown from a car into a hotel used by immigrants. In Turin, the police battled against immigrants.

- April 1990. Four immigrants were murdered in Pescopagano by a local Camorra clan attacking the more recently arrived 'black Mafia' of drug dealers.

- Ten Africans were murdered over a 15-month period in the Caserta area.

In March 1990 thousands of immigrants who had been refused accommodation in Rome had to sleep under bridges. About 1,500 were reported to have been taking turns of four hours each to sleep in parts of the catacombs.[1]

Racial harassment, abuse and attacks have become almost an everyday occurrence for significant numbers of black and ethnic minority people in Italy today. The issue is one of the most serious problems they face.

In February 1994 the Roman Coordination of Immigrants organisation complained that '...entire areas of the centre of the city, the suburbs and coastal towns, are now dominated by terror. We appeal to Major Rutelli and

---

1. *Migration News Sheet*, April 1990

the city institutions to grant us the protection of UN troops.' They also demanded justice and security 'like all the other citizens'.[2]

In Florence and Venice there have been protests that the African beggars on the streets are keeping 'good' tourists, especially Americans, away. A group called 'the undefended citizens of Florence' claimed it did not want the city to become like New York.

This explosion of racist episodes has been caused by the absence of political will to tackle the situation, the non-existence of reception programmes, and the inhuman conditions in which immigrants are forced to live, paying exorbitant rents for huts or rooms shared with dozens of others. Some episodes are triggered by fear, some by selfishness, some by misinformation.

The term 'racism' is not used clearly or consistently in Italy. It is confused with chauvinism, xenophobia, and prejudice, and some national newspapers write of 'racism' against the handicapped, against smokers and even against the elderly. The framework of rejection is based upon many inter-related, mixed taboos and prejudices: against Gypsies, homosexuals, drug addicts, atheists and, in northern Italy, against *terroni*, people from southern Italy and Sicily.

Southerners have long had to face hostility in the north. In June 1989 a southern Italian migrant was beaten to death by a group of northerners. An opinion poll carried out shortly afterwards indicated that two-thirds of people in the north disliked the southerners.[3]

Rising racism towards blacks or extracommunitari (that is third-country nationals, people from outside the European Community, a polite term for Arabs and black Africans) has exacerbated the internal friction, the prejudice against southerners: 'We had to put up with the *terroni* for a long time: you should not ask us now to put up with the blacks too. Go away Bedouins, go away *terroni*'.

Since 1989 racist leaflets issued by newly-formed groups such as Ludwig, Falange and Brigata Goebbels have appeared. The last-named urged vigilance against '... blacks, gypsy pigs, drug traffickers and the filthy Bolsheviks who protect them'.[4]

## THE EXTENT OF THE PROBLEM

In my talks with representatives of the Ministry of the Interior, the City Council, the judiciary and prosecuting authorities, a large number of interviewees expressed concern about the number of racist attacks since the early 1980s. They believed these attacks were increasing and were signs of increasing intolerance. But my requests for data, or for some analysis of this worrying phenomenon, were met mostly by a defensive, non-committal,

---

2. *L'Unita*, 24 February 1994.

3. *Liberation*, 17 July 1989.

4. *Migration News Sheet*, April 1990.

uninterested or uninformed attitude: 'Yes, it's a worrying phenomenon, but we have no data, you should go to the Ministry of the Interior.'

I go there, only to be told that it is the Ministry of Justice which should have such data. And there the response to the lack of monitoring of immigration laws was: 'Why should we be worrying about a few gangs of youths going wild on weekends?'

Most officials assumed that my requests for data were actually criticisms of their actions. There appeared to be little idea of cooperation with colleagues in other relevant departments. A spokesperson from Ostia police station asked: 'Is it not the job of the police to apprehend criminals straight away? Well, we have been really quick to do that on many occasions here in Ostia.' These crimes, he said, were mostly committed by disenchanted youths from underprivileged backgrounds. Considering their families' situations and the very deprived areas where they lived, they could not be blamed greatly for acts of violence which were a form of revenge against a system that has failed them. Dr Roberto Thomas of the Juvenile Court in Rome told me that, because Italy is a Catholic country:

> ... it is based upon a judicial system which tends to forgive youngsters under age, mostly considered not fully responsible ... so it cannot show many convictions for racially motivated crime.

Ms Anna Jacomini, a social worker at the juvenile court, expressed the view that:

> ... even if there was the will to work with other agencies involved, we are not allocated the necessary time or resources. We are just dealing with one crisis after another; quite often we feel completely isolated, lacking managerial support. Our managers are busy fighting to keep the service running in the face of many staff cuts and heavy workloads.

Disillusionment, despondency and lack of direction were evident in most of the agencies I visited. Many congratulated themselves that their services were still running at all. As Dr Raffaele Clemente at police headquarters said:

> With the system cracking up under our feet, the very little which is done to apprehend perpetrators of racially motivated violence is due to the goodwill of individual police officers. But, centrally, there are no guidelines, and no procedures are laid down for recording racially motivated violence.

In these circumstances, it is obviously impossible to obtain reliable data on the extent of the problem. Such figures as I eventually succeeded in obtaining from official sources were internally inconsistent and contradicted each other.

Dottoressa Passannanti of the Ministry of Justice gave me some figures from public prosecutors' offices throughout Italy. They covered the period 1991-93, before the most recent law, the Mancino law (see pp 108-10), had come into force, and dealt with racial, religious, national or ethnic discrimination. Her data indicate very low figures for offences. She did not know how the information had been collected and she had nothing more up-to-date.

Dottoressa Manuguerra of the Ministry of the Interior provided completely different data showing that since the approval of the Mancino law in 1993 there had been 28 arrests and 554 searches by warrant. Another informant in the Ministry of the Interior, Mauro Valeri, also collected information on racially motivated crime, but Dottoressa Manuguerra criticised its validity. Mauro Valeri is in charge of the National Observatory on Xenophobia, the government department responsible for dealing with right-wing terrorism. She told me that her office gathered information on racially motivated crime incidentally in its work on extreme right groups: it did not have specific expertise on racial violence as such.

Altogether, the figures obtained from these Ministries were of little help. There is no central office for recording racial violence, and there are no clear guidelines or procedures for doing so. The information obtained from various sources suggests that any official figures represent a massive underestimate of racially motivated crime.

## WHY ROME?

This report aims to analyse the phenomenon of racist crime in Rome in the context of contemporary Italian social, political and cultural life, with emphasis on the following issues:

- police response to racially motivated crime; the reporting of crimes and apprehension of perpetrators; and police liaison with other agencies

- the role of the prosecuting authorities in the punishment of perpetrators

- the work of relevant statutory and voluntary agencies on immigration matters generally and on racially motivated crime specifically.

The evidence has been gathered through interviews with police officers, judges, public prosecutors, lawyers, journalists, politicians, members of statutory and voluntary organisations, and individual immigrants in their homes, places of worship and makeshift accommodation. National and local newspapers and other publications have also been consulted. Rome was chosen because the worst figures for racial violence in Italy come from that city.

It is generally agreed, however, that racial violence is underreported. It is a recent phenomenon in Italian society and has only just come to the attention of policy-makers. The structures for reporting and prosecuting it are embryonic. Despite awareness of the potentially explosive situation, there is uncertainty, lack of training, and little will to implement the few existing laws in an environment where the presence of immigrants is more a cause for panic than acceptance. The lack of resources, guidelines and structures, combined with incompetence, lack of accountability, and secrecy, are evident across the spectrum of the agencies dealing with racially motivated crime, as will appear below. Most of the information about trials, for example, comes from newspapers, as Italian public prosecutors are difficult to approach. Many officials could be reached only after many letters of recommendation and an introduction by their superiors had been obtained.

## THE ROMAN SOCIAL BACKGROUND

Rome is a great urban centre with many suburbs which are all part of its identity: Ostia, Anzio, Fiumicino and the Castelli. The surrounding region of Lazio will also be mentioned in this report. The city itself is too well known historically and internationally to need much description. Today it is the centre of government, the third largest industrial centre in Italy, and the destination of millions of tourists from all over the world.

In all the research on immigration carried out since the early 1980s, Rome has been identified as one of the most socially complex areas. Over 180 nationalities are represented among the immigrants, of whom 34.7 per cent are from Europe, 30.8 per cent from Africa, 17.7 per cent from Asia and 16.1 per cent from America. Most are young (71.7 per cent are between 19 and 40 years old) and over half (57 per cent) are men. Most come to Rome to look for work. About 14,000 *extracommunitari* are in employment, mainly engaged in the 'black economy' (that is unofficial, unregulated, non-taxpaying work). Italians were working in the black economy long before large-scale immigration began, but now the immigrants are doing jobs that Italians are no longer willing to do: building, cleaning, heavy industry including textiles and metal engineering, as well as seasonal work in the countryside.

Sixteen thousand *extracommunitari* are registered as unemployed in Rome. However, it is difficult to make accurate estimates for employment and unemployment because a large proportion of Italy's immigrants are clandestine. As they are not legally resident, and as they then work – if at all – unofficially, and are ineligible for most benefits, clandestine immigrants do not show up in many official figures.

Research carried out in Rome in May 1994 by the Instituto Placido Martini in collaboration with 16 immigrant organisations showed an alarming situation. Interviews were conducted with 276 immigrants of 32 nationalities, and 36 per cent of them had no residence permit. Many had been forced into unofficial jobs as labourers, street pedlars, window cleaners, waiters, dishwashers and domestic workers. Most found Rome a very difficult city to live in, and felt that their rights were not safeguarded. Their worst problem was housing: some were living in cellars, huts, containers, caravans or cars, but most were in rooms shared with others, sometimes ten people to a room. One-third lived in accommodation without a kitchen.

It is estimated by the Catholic welfare organisation Caritas that 10,000 *extracommunitari* in Rome are homeless, living on the streets.[5] Certainly, large numbers of them barely survive. As hardship increases, the indigenous population grows more and more frightened of the poor, according to Monsignor Di Liegro, director of Caritas Diocesana.[6]

---

5. *Dossiere statistico*, 1993.

6. *La Repubblica*, 5 November 1993.

I visited several makeshift settlements in disused or demolished buildings and abandoned factories where immigrants were hidden away and just managing to survive. Urban degradation and deprivation are found in many districts of the city, in sharp contrast to the great wealth in other quarters. In Rome, the contradictions and problems of Italian society in general are very noticeable. The city is crippled by corruption, mismanagement and lack of any clear policies or guidelines on legal procedures. Rome is administered by a coalition formed after the municipal elections of April 1994. The parties concerned are the PDS (Partito Democratico della Sinistra, formed from the old Communist Party of Italy), the Greens, and the Movimento Sociale Italiano (MSI), a neo-fascist party which is part of the Alleanza Nazionale (National Alliance). These long-term opponents find it difficult to agree with each other, but the Italian electoral system has forced them into partnership. Older established parties, particularly the Socialists and Christian Democrats, were disbanded after corruption charges were brought against several of their members in 1993 and 1994.

Immigration is a hot potato. All new proposals for projects to help immigrants, usually presented by the Greens or the PDS, get voted down by Alleanza Nazionale. Even when public money is allocated for projects like settlement centres it rarely reaches them. There is institutional immobility and chaos amid continuous allegations of fraud, theft and squandering. For four years, no money has been received for problems posed by immigration. Many of the people I interviewed in the few paid positions available in the voluntary sector had not been paid for months; some had not been paid since their employment began – the money promised had been used to clear the deficit in other sectors. Some were taking their employers to court. Among refugees I interviewed, I found that some had never received the daily allowance of 35,000 lire (about £14) they were entitled to under the provisions of the Martelli law. Nobody knew where the money had gone. Similarly, international funds allocated by the United Nations Human Rights Committee for refugee welfare had never reached refugees. This was confirmed both by the refugee organisations and by individuals.

There are over 200 voluntary organisations, some secular and some religious, working for or with immigrants in Rome. These are in addition to public bodies. They provide a good example of the kind of work carried out in the nation at large. The main bases of the major political parties, the trade unions, the Catholic Church and a number of immigrant organisations are also found in Rome, as is the National Observatory on Xenophobia, the only organisation which specifically gathers evidence on racially motivated crime.

## IMMIGRATION

Throughout the twentieth century until the 1980s Italy was a country of emigration rather than immigration. Like other European states, it had always received some European settlers, but these were vastly outnumbered by the millions of Italians who moved to settle elsewhere.

From outside Europe, small numbers of Chinese came during the inter-war period and also in the 1960s. Political refugees arrived in the 1960s and 1970s, most of them from Chile and other Latin American dictatorships. Refugee intellectuals and dissidents were warmly welcomed.

A study by the trade union Ecap Enim showed that large numbers of women from the Philippines, Cape Verde, Mauritius, Sri Lanka, Eritrea, Somalia and Nigeria were working as housemaids in well-to-do homes in Italy. According to Caritas Diocesana they began coming in the 1970s. Hidden from view in domestic work they did not provoke the kind of racial attacks and demonstrations that black male migrants were to suffer later.[7] What they experienced instead was sexual stereotyping:

> Up until recently, for the young Italian male, going with a black woman was considered to be the ultimate.[8]

Italy's rapid economic growth in the post-war decades drew large numbers of workers from Sicily and southern Italy to northern industrial towns, and immigrants from the Maghreb countries of north Africa began to move in, particularly as seasonal workers, to meet the shortage of agricultural workers in the south. In Italy generally, African immigrants from former Italian colonies had been a familiar sight for some time, but in small numbers. In the 1980s these appeared to be increasing, but there was no reliable data. No major immigration law had been passed in Italy since before the Second World War, and most of the immigrants were unofficial and unrecorded.

In the late 1970s many Yugoslavs were admitted to work in the building trade after a great earthquake in Friuli, in the north, had devastated a large area. This foreshadowed a movement from eastern Europe which was to grow after 1989.

The national census of 1971 showed that there were 121,116 foreign workers resident in Italy. In 1981 the figure was 210,937. These figures refer to people legally permitted to reside and work in Italy. But it was evident by the late 1980s that hundreds of thousands of non-Europeans had entered Italy. Employers in the south were sometimes happy to use this large pool of unofficial labour for casual, low-paid work in agriculture. Cities were the preferred destination for immigrants, but they found on arrival that there too they had to take very low-paid work or to spend their days on the street as pedlars. Illegal immigration was not all spontaneous, some of it was actively organised by criminal organisations. In 1991 Mohideen Nowfer, president of the Sri Lankan Immigrants' Association, condemned the shameful exploitation of immigration by criminal organisations which, 'with false promises encourage illegal entry and demand from their unfortunate victims money equivalent to 15 years' income in our country'.

7. Andall, 1990.

8. *L'Espresso*, 3 July 1988, p.9.

In 1995 the former Minister of Social Affairs, Mr F Contri, expressed alarm:

> The organisations which manage the labour traffic are now really powerful. Magistrates confirm this. Often, we have slavery. We know of people who have been made to enter Italy travelling in false compartments in lorries, of women transported in cages and made to become prostitutes, and a horrendous traffic in workers in which, in some cases, Italian civil servants could also be involved.

Exploitation of immigrants had already been happening in the late 1980s, but was not publicised. Immigration only became a central political question in 1989. At the same time, racial violence too became a matter of public concern: the two issues were interlinked.

Trade unions and church organisations had long been concerned at the exploitation of illegal entrants and wanted something done to regularise the situation. Government officials were worried about organised crime. Workers and shopkeepers in northern cities were complaining about the effects of illegal immigration on their jobs and trade. In August 1989 an African immigrant, Jerry Maslo, was murdered, and the story received extensive media coverage. Incidents of racial violence became hot news. A massive anti-racist demonstration took place in Rome in October 1989. A new immigration law was proposed by the government, with the aim of cutting down illegal entry, helping illegal immigrants already present to regularise their status, and establishing clear procedures for receiving immigrants and securing rights for them. This proposal, which became the Martelli law, was supported by the main political parties, and was opposed only by the (right-wing) Republicans and the (neo-fascist) MSI. It was hoped that the measure would reduce racial hatred and violence, both by reducing entry and by improving immigrants' rights so that their labour would not be exploited.

The Martelli law came into force in 1990. It was entitled *Urgent Provisions Regarding Political Asylum, the Entry and Residence of non-EC nationals, and the Regularisation of non-EC nationals and Stateless Persons already Present in Italian Territory.* Until 1989 Italy had recognised only east Europeans as refugees. The Martelli law granted refugee status to non-Europeans 'under the warrant of the United Nations High Commissioner for Refugees', and reorganised the procedures for examining asylum claims. Asylum seekers entering Italy were to get an allowance of 35,000 lire a day for 45 days. They were required to have presented their claims to the frontier police. Asylum seekers who had arrived before the new law was in force were to apply to police headquarters.

The report by Mr Contri, Minister for Social Affairs in 1993, said that only 145 asylum requests out of 1,564 had been granted, and only 1,700 asylum seekers had received the specified initial allowance while awaiting a decision. The Italian Refugee Council, reporting on the same year, said that 7,475 asylum applications had been sent to the police but that most or all of these applications had not been sent on to the Ministry of the Interior for

9. *La Repubblica*, March 1995.

decision. A total of 26,617 residence permits were issued in 1993 to Somalis and Yugoslavs, although they were not granted UN refugee status. (The Geneva Convention's terms are too narrow to include fugitives from civil war or starvation.) They were granted instead exceptional leave to remain under Decree-Law 390/92, which gave them, for a year at a time, rights to work, reside and obtain medical assistance. The Decree-Law covered only those Yugoslavs who had entered Italy after June 1991, not those who had come in earlier as temporary workers but were unable to go back because of the war. The Decree-Law was passed in a rush because of the public outcry about the inhuman conditions in which Somalis were living in the big cities, and because of the sudden landing of many Yugoslavs on the Adriatic coast. The war in Yugoslavia also impelled the movement of many Gypsies into Italy. They were accommodated in camps scattered across Italy, which became targets for arson attacks by some local people.

For ordinary immigrants (that is, other than asylum seekers and other fugitives) the Martelli law laid down new rules and procedures for non-EC nationals. With the exception of tourists, entrants had to apply to the police within eight days of entry for a residence permit, which would be valid for two years and renewable for a further two years, provided that the applicant could show he or she had a job and a fixed abode. The law also provided for people already present in Italy to regularise their status by application to the police, and authorised expulsion orders against people whose status was irregular.

In practice, the new immigration law did not achieve its purpose: many failed to apply to regularise their status, and those who did found that the police often either failed to process their applications or imposed unduly difficult conditions for acceptance.

Of 245,000 two-year residence permits obtained when the law was first introduced, only 185,000 were renewed in 1992. According to Italia Razzismo (1994), 60,000 people had either already been repatriated or forced back into clandestine status because they could not get renewals. In 1994 the Ministry of the Interior sent circulars to police stations instructing them that proof of employment was no longer needed and that permits were to be issued for four years. However, in Rome only one-fifth of residence permits were renewed. In contravention of the circulars' instructions, four-year renewals were issued only if the applicant presented a contract of work or a certificate of registration in the unemployment lists. A two-year renewal was given to anyone formerly unemployed and currently working, or formerly working and currently unemployed. Furthermore, police insisted on seeing tenancy agreements, which were usually impossible to obtain. Most landlords refused to issue contracts because they wanted to avoid paying taxes. And, of course, many immigrants had no fixed abode.

The government claimed that the laws were successful in reducing irregular immigration because there were so few renewals in 1994. In fact the rate for regularising immigrants is far lower now than when immigrants obtained their initial permits just after the law came into force. According to Dino Frisullo from the organisation Senzaconfine, immigrants who have been left without residence permits have no rights and are forced into hiding for fear of expulsion, and victims of racist crimes cannot complain because they would then face removal.

The Martelli law provided for 39 information centres to be set up at the principal border points. These have never been established, and the acceptance or refusal of foreigners at the borders is left completely in the hands of the border police, who are very often unprepared for such a task.[10]

There was an attempt in December 1994 to legislate further on immigration. A Bill promoted by the MSI and Northern League (see page 24) proposed limiting entry to those who could show at the port of entry that they already had work and accommodation arranged, and making it a criminal offence to enter illegally or to be responsible for another person's illegal entry. The Bill would have penalised employers of illegal labour and landlords charging excessive rents for overcrowded accommodation. It would also have introduced magnetic identity cards to replace existing paper residence permits and the requirement for an entrant to have a medical card certifying that the bearer was not a danger to public health. There were provisions for holding people in reception centres while their identity was verified, and for speeding up expulsion procedures. The proposals caused an uproar on the left and were strongly opposed by the many lay and religious organisations which offer assistance and support to immigrants. The Bill was not passed because the prime minister, Silvio Berlusconi, fell from office on 22 December 1994 soon after its introduction.

Meanwhile, the Martelli law had not been properly implemented. In the absence of circulars instructing the police on how to operate it, enormous differences in behaviour were documented by Italia Razzismo. The various *Questura* (police headquarters) accepted different documentary evidence of work and abode. The same variations in use of discretion were found at border posts.

## ANTI-RACIST LAW

On 19 December 1992 the Italian government submitted to parliament Bill No.2061/C. It introduced urgent measures on racial, ethnic and religious discrimination and was aimed at preventing and repressing xenophobic or anti-semitic intolerance and violence. The Bill became Decree-Law No.122 on 26 April 1993, and came into force two days later. It is known as the Mancino law, and provides that:

> Any organisation, association, movement or group with aims that include incitement to discrimination, to hatred or to violence on racial, ethnic, national or religious grounds shall be prohibited. Anyone who participates in such organisations, associations, movements or groups or assists in their activities shall be punished, for the mere fact of such participation or assistance, by one to five years' imprisonment. The penalties shall be increased for the leaders and promoters of such organisations, associations or groups.

---

10. Italia Razzismo, 1994.

Article 2 extends the penalties which Italy applies to Mafia-type criminal activities to persons who are:

> ... to be considered as members of associations, movements or groups which advocate, threaten or use violence for the purpose of ethnic, racial or religious discrimination or hatred,

and to persons who:

> ... in the course of public meetings show signs or display the customary or self-created emblems or symbols of associations, movements or groups with aims that include incitement to violence, discrimination or hatred on ethnic, national, racial or religious grounds.

Article 3 increased the penalty by one-third:

> ... for offences committed for the purposes of ethnic, national, racial or religious discrimination or hatred, or with the aim of facilitating the activity of associations, movements or groups whose objectives include these purposes.

Article 5 authorises searches, seizures and, in the event of a court sentence, confiscation of immovable property, when the perpetrator of one of the offences involving racial discrimination or hatred 'has used it as a meeting place, or as a store or place of refuge', as well as the search for, confiscation and seizure of:

> ... emblems, symbols or propaganda materials made by or customary to associations, movements or groups whose aim is, *inter alia*, incitement to violence or hatred on ethnic, national, racial or religious grounds.

Article 6 contains procedural provisions and lays down that, for the offences covered by Article 3, official proceedings must be taken in all cases. Article 7 provides that, in specific cases, when 'there are good reasons to believe that the activity of associations, movements or groups favours the perpetration' of racial offences, the association, movement or group may be suspended or even dissolved and its property confiscated.

The offence of racist propaganda had already been the subject of court applications and interpretation. Particular mention should be made of the ruling by the Supreme Court of Cassation on 16 January 1986 which stated in connection with defamation in the press and racist propaganda, that the local Jewish communities and the union of these communities had the right to be regarded as 'passive subjects and injured parties in respect of the offence of defamation in the press of the Jewish community'. Moreover:

> ... this right may be recognised in respect of an individual belonging to the Jewish race, since the common interest of the Jewish community, unlike the general interest, which by nature is indivisible, may be divided and considered on an individual basis.

In the same ruling, the Court of Cassation specified that, in the case of:

> ... an offence against all persons belonging to the Jewish race taken indiscriminately and individually, a fundamental right of the individual is inevitably involved, namely

the right of honour and reputation, which is guaranteed by article two of the Constitution as part of the inviolable rights of persons viewed first and foremost as individuals before being considered as members of social groups within which the individual personality develops.

The 1992 law, even if reasonably comprehensive, suffers from a big gap between its provisions and its implementation.

At a press conference at the Chamber of Deputies on 19 August 1994, the Green/PDS MP, Alfonso Pecoraro Scanio, condemned this failure 'in the light of a recrudescence of racist crimes. There is a law which is totally not applied.' He asked the government to refer the matter to the Justice Commission. Under the law passed a year earlier there had been, he said, only a few trials, very few sentences, and very few extra sentences given for the aggravating circumstances of racist motives. He also called for an investigation in all the public prosecutors' offices.[11]

The law, he said, also provided for additional or alternative punishments: voluntary work in the community for a period of from one to 12 weeks; returning home at fixed times; suspension of driving licence; prohibition from voting or taking part in political activities. But, said Mr Scanio, the government had not yet decided on the modalities of work in the community:

> We should send the perpetrators of racially motivated crime to clean the camps where the immigrants live instead of sending them home, thanks to the suspended sentence.[12]

It was reported in the same newspaper that Loretta Caponi, president of the Forum of Foreign Communities in Italy, had complained that the Mancino law, as well as providing legal tools for the repression of racially motivated crime – which were not applied – had included preventive measures, which were also never implemented:

> The educational initiatives for offenders are non-existent; so is the training for teachers and civil servants ... the government also needs to control and encourage local authorities because they are often responsible for the poor and inhuman conditions in which immigrants live, as well as for the failure to apply the law.

Like the Martelli law, the Mancino law has failed to safeguard the rights of immigrants. As Italia Razzismo commented in 1995:

> Every law turns out to be another shot in the dark, dictated by emergencies, devised in panic and implemented in chaos.

## THE ROLE OF THE EXTREME RIGHT AND ELECTORAL POLITICS

Organisations on the extreme right have been active in Italy for decades. As in other countries, their membership often overlaps, and there are links

---

11. ANSA – National Press Agency.

12. *Il Mattino*, August 1994.

between some of the people active in 'respectable' politics and more sinister, sometimes terrorist, groups.

Italy's neo-fascist party, the MSI, was led at first by Giorgio Almirante, formerly one of Mussolini's ministers. One of its members, Massimo Abbatangelo, who was accused of involvement in the 1985 bombing of a train near Florence in which 17 people were killed and more than 200 injured, became, in the early 1990s, a member of the Italian parliament.

> Like Abbatangelo, most of Italy's notorious right-wing terrorists started in the MSI before moving on to such groups as Ordine Nuovo and the Nuclei Armati Rivoluzionari (NAR) which bombed Bologna railway station in August 1980 killing 86 people.[13]

The Italian general election of March 1994 produced a government which was a precarious three-way alliance between media tycoon Silvio Berlusconi, MSI leader Gianfranco Fini and the wayward rebel, Umberto Bossi, leader of the Northern League. Right-wing candidates romped home in Lazio, the region surrounding the city of Rome. Fini's MSI had made great gains in southern Italy. In 1993 he had only narrowly missed victory in the mayoral elections in Rome, while his 'sidekick' Alessandra Mussolini was similarly narrowly defeated in Naples. Fini presented himself as a moderate to some voters, but in early April 1993 he had praised Mussolini as the greatest statesman of all time, as a sop to the hardline Movimento Politico, whose members had been demonstrating in the streets with fascist salutes and screams of 'Duce, Duce!'.[14]

Throughout the election campaign of 1994 immigration was an emotive issue. All the parties addressed it in their manifestos. The Northern League made it a major issue: it wanted redirection of funds from immigrant settlement centres towards care of the indigenous elderly, the removal of immigrants' street stalls, and controls introduced on windscreen cleaners at traffic lights (invariably immigrants). The League MP Irene Pivetti proposed careful selection of immigrants, and that those who had neither work nor a home should be expelled.[15] New entry should be stopped. The MSI wanted a five-year halt to immigration; during that time an immigrant census would be taken and all immigrants not in work would be expelled. The MSI linked these proposals to demands for better living conditions in sending countries, to be achieved through aid to Third World countries.

Mr Buontempo, the victorious MSI candidate in Ostia, the Roman district with the highest number of racist attacks, said that immigration was a public order problem, to be managed by police headquarters:

> In society there must be order and hierarchy, immigrants must go home and there must be a curfew at night-time, with no noise anywhere, especially in the *centri sociali*.

These *centri sociali* are left-wing youth clubs which, particularly on the

---

13. Committee of Inquiry on Racism and Xenophobia, European Parliament, 1991.

14. *La Repubblica*, April 1994.

15. *Ibid.*

periphery of Rome, organise cultural, educational and training activities for local unemployed youth. They are run entirely by volunteers in disused buildings, which they claim in the name of the right of the local population to be free from racism and marginalisation. They aim to change the life of the outer suburbs where young people feel unable to escape and are offered nothing but unemployment.

The left-wing parties in the election found it difficult to discuss immigration, for fear of losing electoral support. They made a general appeal to the ideal of a future multiracial society, and proposed some regulation of entry, yearly programming to help immigrants out of the black economy and to facilitate the creation of cooperatives, extension of social and economic rights for immigrants, the right to vote in local elections, and reform of asylum law to include fugitives from wars. The left (the PDS and its allies) did badly throughout northern and southern Italy, retaining only the old communist bastions of Tuscany, Umbria and Emilia Romagna. Berlusconi's alliance, which included his own free market party, Forza Italia, the free market and anti-immigrant Northern League, and the state-control, anti-immigrant MSI, took power. It was an uneasy coalition and the government fell after eight months. Meanwhile, however, anti-immigrant feeling had been encouraged.

In May 1994, one year after the Mancino law was passed, 200 skinheads singing the praises of nazism and fascism held a procession in Vicenza, in the north. The police did not prohibit the demonstration, but simply put a cordon round the black-shirted demonstrators, who for more than two hours chanted slogans like 'We are the heirs of Salo' (the Salo Republic represented one of the most brutal interludes in the history of Italian fascist rule, and was explicitly anti-semitic) and tried to set fire to immigrant homes. Skinheads had come from all over Italy and were led by the head of the youth section of MSI. It was a significant occasion because it represented a clear breach of the Mancino anti-racist law and also of the constitutional provision forbidding the re-establishment of the fascist party. One can only assume that the election campaign and the change of government had helped to create the climate for such a large-scale demonstration and also for the police indifference to it: the head of the police and the new Interior Minister, a Northern League MP, had let it happen.

Earlier, in 1992, Mr Parisi, chief of police, had said that 1,100 'naziskins' (skinheads on the extreme right) had been recorded throughout Italy. The Roman right-wing Movimento Politico had mobilised Milan and Venice skinheads in February to march with them along Mussolini's old route, and two months later Meridiano Zero, a skinhead group with a branch in the southern outskirts of Rome, had demonstrated under a balcony in Venice from which Mussolini had spoken. One month later the MSI banner was used in a similar demonstration. Such activities were clearly intended by the Mancino law to be banned: in fact just after the law was passed a police operation had closed branches of 'naziskin' groups all over Italy, seizing banners, clubs and busts of Mussolini and arresting leading figures in a few major groups. However, after the general election of 1994, the banning of 'naziskins' appears to have stopped. The implications for the struggle against racially motivated crime are obvious.

In autumn 1994 there were local elections. Many MSI candidates were successful in the Rome area. In Ostia they campaigned in the style of Le Pen, the leader of the French Front National. Ostia includes the largest area of decaying and derelict housing in Rome. It is a refuge for impoverished commuters, people with housing problems and immigrants, many of whom live in semi-ruined, disused buildings on the coast, where they were forced to go after being evacuated forcibly by the police from a disused pasta factory in Pantanella. MSI also won in Ladispoli, near Rome, after campaigning against Russian and Polish immigrants. Some of the local MSI candidates were young people, extremist football fans. Their hero is Mr T Buontempo, MP for Ostia, who crusades against criminals, drug traffickers and thieves (all identified by him as immigrants).

A major question in the local elections was the siting of Gypsy camps. An attack on a Gypsy camp, with about 300 people, including some MSI district councillors and some Ostian citizens, taking part in it, was watched by the police, who did nothing to intervene. The reception camp, which the municipality had started to fit out, was badly damaged.

Violence against Gypsies increased in 1994 and 1995. The most horrific incident took place in Pisa in March 1995. A man in a car gave two Gypsy children a gift-box which then exploded in their faces. One child lost an eye and had to have his face and hands reconstructed with plastic surgery. The other lost most fingers on both hands. Three young men were arrested for this offence and large quantities of explosives and weapons were found in their homes. Two were given suspended sentences of one year and ten months, and the other an eight months' suspended sentence.

During 1994 and in the first two weeks of 1995 there were more than 125 attacks against Gypsy camps located on the outskirts of major Italian industrial cities. These camps lack even elementary hygienic services, have no light or heating, and are surrounded by mud and rubbish. But whenever it is proposed to fit out a camp with the necessary services, the plan is stopped by the parties of the right. The policy of the MSI in Rome is to drive all Gypsies outside the ring road.

After the general election, the hardline right-wing Movimento Politico played a prominent role in developing local Alleanza Nazionale strategy. Its leader, M Boccacci, held a political rally at Tor de Cenci just after the skinhead march in Vicenza (see p.112) to oppose the municipality's plans to set up a Gypsy reception centre there. Fascist squads kept a vigilant eye on proceedings. The 'naziskins' in Rome have been emboldened since the 1994 elections to attack the left-wing *centri sociali* in Rome.

A few right-wing Catholics have aligned themselves with the neo-fascists, saying, 'Our enemies are Jews and communists'. In 1994 this fraction joined the Movimento Politico in an anti-abortion coalition, distributing leaflets describing abortion as a 'threat to the survival of the white race'.

# IMPLEMENTATION OF ANTI-RACIST LAW

## Sentences

It was difficult to obtain data on the sentences imposed under the anti-racist laws, but the following six examples give a flavour of court practice.

- 13 May 1990. A bus driver from Bologna was fined 600,000 lire (about £250) for insults and ordered to pay one million lire (£400) as compensation for having told two Senegalese: 'Dirty negroes, we will send you all to your own country'. The bus driver was convinced that they had no bus tickets.

- 25 February 1992. The judge of a lower court in Bologna granted a Tunisian one million lire as compensation for having failed in his application for employment.

- 18 April 1992. In the Criminal Court of Rome, A Insabato was sentenced to one year and six months' imprisonment because during the Lazio v. Torino football match he had burned a Jewish religious flag displaying the Star of David. This is one of the few instances of a court applying the 1975 law, which punishes 'whoever instigates discrimination of any kind or violent acts against people solely because they belong to a national, ethnic or racial group'.

- 20 June 1995. In Vicenza, P Puschiavo, founder of Veneto Fronte Skin (which organised the march on Vicenza), was sentenced to two years and one month in prison, together with the co-founder of the group, I Da Deppo, for 'instigation of racial hatred'. Three other defendants were sentenced to one year and six months, and a further three to one year. (They represented the 'wild group' of the neo-Nazi wing of the Venetian right, which also comprises the group of F Freda, now awaiting trial, and some 'fundamentalist' Catholic groups.) The public prosecutor had very hard words for the eight skinheads, and the judge accepted that they had glorified ideas and racist actions typical of the disbanded Fascist Party; this was evident also from the books and videos they had circulated.

- 28 May 1995. An exemplary sentence of two years' imprisonment was passed on 11 'naziskins' for a racist raid on two immigrants, surprised in their sleep and seriously wounded in Colle Oppio.

- 18 April 1992. Four youngsters in Bologna had thrown incendiary bottles into a group of huts where North Africans lived. They were sentenced to seven years for manslaughter, but on appeal they were found guilty only of damage and of carrying petrol bombs, and the sentences were reduced to three years and three months.

Very few sentences have been imposed, considering the number of alleged racist attacks recorded by the National Observatory on Xenophobia. Moreover, very few cases are actually reported to the police. Those that are produce lengthy investigations, which often end in suspended or negotiated sentences, on evidence which may never have been heard in court. The Italian courts favour forgiveness rather than punishment when very young defendants are involved. As Dr Thomas, Assistant Public Prosecutor at the Juvenile Court, put it:

> After all, we are in a Catholic country where the family, or rather the children, are the pillars. If we judge them criminal at a young age, what will happen to them afterwards?

And Dr Clemente from DIGOS said:

> I know there are few sentences, and many of them are suspended, but our prisons are so full and there are so few who re-offend.

### Processes for reporting, investigating and prosecuting racially motivated crime

Both Dr Clemente of DIGOS and Dr D'Angelo, head of the Ostia police, were full of praise for the celerity with which perpetrators of racially motivated crime are usually apprehended. Their views were borne out by the files I consulted, which were 600 pages long. Each file covered a full investigation by the police and the public prosecutor's office, with documentary evidence and often with handwritten reports, meticulously recording all the details. Racially motivated crime is not reported on special forms or described in different terminology from other crimes.

The pattern emerging from these files was that racist crimes were drawn to the attention of the police by passers-by or other witnesses at bus-stops or in trains. It was rare for a victim to report a crime. Some newspaper articles have asserted that victims fail to understand that in Italy they have the right to report a crime against them to police. I found no files recording arson or desecration of places of worship, nor of reported crimes where the perpetrators had not been caught.

### Case study: Noamani Faycal

The file is that of the criminal proceedings for the racist attack against Noamani Faycal, and is typical as far as the modalities of the attack are concerned: the number and age of the perpetrators, location, line of investigation, procedures and, most of all, the sentence imposed.

I present first the facts as stated by the plaintiff's suit of action presented in the Public Prosecutor's Office of the Magistrate's Court of Rome:

Mr Noamani Faycal, born 28/02/1968 in Tunisia states: on the evening of 03/09/1993 at around 9.30 while I was walking I was attacked by three people while two others were holding me from the back with an arm around my neck. I later identified one of them as C D'Onghia. It was him that stabbed me in the chest, on the right side, above my lung while saying 'you are dead, you are finished'. My hand got cut and later needed 10 stitches when I stopped the second stabbing with that hand. Meanwhile a citizen, passing in a car turned on the headlights dazzling the attackers who fled.

I was bleeding but managed to reach a nearby bar where my brother, Mr S Noamani was. I described to him what had happened. He went where the young men usually gather and there he found Mr D'Onghia, who, together with the other two who were later arrested, hurled themselves against him. They stopped when they saw two *carabinieri* walking towards them. These *carabinieri* had been told by the other bar's customers about what had happened. I was accompanied by the *carabinieri* to a nearby doctor, who examined me and gave me urgent treatment and issued a certificate for the *carabiniere*. I was then taken to the hospital where I remained as a patient until 12/09/1993. On discharge from the hospital two stitches were left in the chest. At the moment I still suffer from the consequence of the injuries and I ask to be compensated for the damages suffered and for my suffering.

With the present formal act I take legal action against Messrs C D'Onghia, M Meneghini, and A Diana. I ask that your Honour should proceed against the same for the crime of injuries against the undersigned and for the crime provided for in the decree-law, N122 of 26/04/1993 for racist acts and for the previous threats before the aggression, in accordance with the procedure laid down by the law.

Therefore I ask that the same are also prosecuted according to the law. The undersigned reserves the right to start civil proceedings. The undersigned also confirms the appointment as Counsel for the Defence of S.C.

One of the first statements is always the one taken by the police officer or *carabiniere* who records the names, dates of birth and general details of the people brought to the police station for questioning and the circumstantial evidence of the crimes of which they are suspected.

All the information is recorded on the police station's headed paper and signed and countersigned by the police officers present (usually one or two). A graphic description of the assault is given, with a verbatim record of what was said; for example: 'You are dead, you are finished, you damned die'. A description of the knife used and a full medical certificate follows:

The medical report certifies a cut in the chest, 2 cm deep and 4 cm long... [all the injuries and the prognosis are specified together with an account of how the blows were inflicted and how long it will take for the victim to recover].

Two sets of evidence are presented and recorded: from the police and from the public prosecutor. The police conduct the preliminary investigation up to the point of arrest, when the public prosecutor is informed of the charges brought so far against the suspects being held in custody. The public prosecutor leads the investigations up to the point where the evidence is considered sufficient and presented to the judge of first instance, who decides on the basis of the evidence whether or not to summon anyone.

In the Faycal case, there were two counts of indictment against the defendants:

- (artt.120-56-57-577 n.4 -61n.5 e art. 3 comma 1 l.25.6.1993 n.205)

  ... in that, acting together, in Campagnano di Roma on 3 September 1993, they had seized N Faycal from behind by his hair and stabbed him in the chest with a knife: that their actions were unequivocally designed to cause the death of the aforementioned N Faycal, and it was through no wish of theirs that the criminal intention did not succeed; that an aggravating circumstance was they acted for trivial reasons, consisting in the disproportion between the motive and the criminal actions, and had acted despicably, considering the immorality of the racial hatred which decided them upon the action. Furthermore these actions had been committed by three persons together attacking a single unarmed person, and by night.

- (art. 4 legge 110/75 -110 C.p. -61 n.2 C.P.)

  ... in that, acting in complicity to commit the above-mentioned crime at the time and place above mentioned, they had unlawfully removed from their house a knife (type unspecified).

The judgement given on 30 November 1994 at Rome's Criminal Court found two of the defendants, Diana and Meneghini, not guilty on both counts. D'Onghia was found guilty of using a weapon to cause harm with criminal intent, with the aggravating circumstance that Noamani Faycal was taken from behind, by surprise, in an unlit alleyway. The court held that the aggravating factor of the law of 25 June 1993, n.205 concerning racial hatred, could not be applied in this case. The insulting epithets and the determination to commit a crime which D'Onghia had not hesitated to express while on his punitive expedition had demonstrated prejudice and a stereotype of racial superiority, but had lacked that deep-rooted hatred tending to cause harm and to overpower others by any means, linked to the denial of respect for human rights, to which the law on racial hatred referred. The defendants' insults had called for 'the sterile closure of the local territory of the polis', a concept which did not fit the level of maturity of youths from the Campagnano. The case had therefore to be considered in the light of the remaining aggravating factors. There could be no doubt of the evil motives behind the actions committed. The pleas of self-defence could not be upheld. However, D'Onghia's action was to strike one blow with a blade. The absence of repeated stabbing meant that homicidal intent could be excluded. It was also necessary to take into account that the trap laid by the three attackers had in fact permitted the Tunisian to escape. The evidence of many young people had shown that the decision to undertake this kind of punitive expedition was not related to the more serious charge brought here.

D'Onghia was given the following sentence: under Article 133 of the Penal Code, one year's imprisonment; under Article 81, the payment of costs of the trial and the expenses of custody. However, taking into account the youth of the defendant, his clean penal record, and his low level of education, which had become apparent during the judge's questioning at the preliminary investigations, he was granted the double benefit of a suspended sentence and non-mention of the sentence on his record, provided that he did not reoffend. He was ordered to pay damages of eight million lire to Noamani Faycal and to pay the costs of the trial.

## The role of the police

The immigrants I interviewed did not trust the police even when they had been victims of crime. Most of their encounters with police officers consisted of the police asking for their residence permits, and they were fearful of being presented with travel orders to leave the country within 15 days if they went to a police station.

Mr Patrick Kouassi of SOS-Racisme told me of two immigrants who had been victims of a beating in a bar in Ostia. They had been insulted and provoked by two local youths and a fight started. Bystanders called the police, who heard the testimony of witnesses present. Although the evidence supported the view that the two youths had started the trouble, the police arrested the immigrants. I tried to find out more about this incident, but the head of the local police denied all knowledge of it.

The only organisation in Rome which provides lawyers to defend immigrants is Senzaconfine. Dino Frisullo, from that organisation, told me that the police were very good at covering their tracks and defending whatever action they had taken; it was almost impossible to get access to their files and very difficult to bring charges against them. Dr Clemente of DIGOS, the police office for special operations in Rome, implicitly confirmed this:

> One must not forget that Italy had formerly a fascist dictatorship in which the police were organised on a military-style, hierarchical basis, playing a fundamental role in controlling and repressing discontent and also conducting investigations and interrogations with summary methods.

Police stations are austere places and the reception is sometimes rude and abrupt. Officers wear guns and visitors go through bag searches and close inspection of documents. It must be remembered, however, that the high level of secrecy and lack of accountability which characterises, in particular, special pools of investigators, is regarded as necessary in order not to jeopardise the fight against terrorism by extreme left and extreme right organisations. There are links between xenophobic, racist and new right organisations and certain terrorist groups. Both Mr Aniasi, Vice-President of the Italian Chamber of Deputies, and Professor Marco Revelli of Turin have pointed to the persistence in some sections of Italian society of a conspiratorial tradition – there were attempted coups in 1964, 1970 and 1974.

There is no special community relations department in the Italian police force, nor any tradition of consulting members of the public or holding meetings with them to plan joint action against crime. The only example I could find of such activity was a police campaign in September 1993. After many complaints of psychological and physical aggression against immigrants in custody, the *Questura* organised a series of meetings with immigrant organisations. Officer F Masone was reported in *La Repubblica* as saying that 'the victims of racial violence must report to the police without the fear of being deported'.

These meetings involved police officers at every level as well as representatives of Caritas and other voluntary organisations which help immigrants.

Mr Masone proposed a direct link between the organisations and himself, a new 24-hour watch in areas of recent attacks, and increased patrols in areas of high risk. More frequent checks on landlords were promised, to verify if fair rents were being charged. Leaflets in various languages were issued to assure victims of racist crimes that they would not be removed from the country before the end of the investigation of a reported crime. The community leaders were invited to report exploitation in the workplace and in housing.

Unfortunately, Mr Masone had left his post before this study was begun, and with him had gone all the information about what happened next. There appeared to have been no follow up action, as the immigrants and their organisations seemed to know nothing about it when questioned.

There have been many examples in Italy generally of police brutality against Gypsies. The worst known incident took place in Bologna, where so-called 'police death squads of the white Fiat Uno' continued for years to terrorise local Gypsy camps, shooting blindly at their caravans, wounding and killing. The 'bandits in uniform of the white Fiat Uno' were convicted in January 1995, and the local newspaper, *Il Resto del Carlino*, expressed suspicions that these officers were:

> ... not the crazy cells of an organism, but the extreme phase of a disease which, with different degrees of seriousness, had struck the entire *Questura*.

Although Bologna's *Questura* is almost certainly not the only one to contain 'crazy cells', there have been very few sentences passed on police officers for such abuses. The two examples I came across in Rome were of a *carabiniere* who had killed a Gypsy child in custody, and another *carabiniere* who had beaten up a Polish refugee accused of theft so severely that the man lost his spleen and, almost, his life. The beating took place in the barracks in Fiumicino and was only brought to the attention of the prosecuting authorities because the victim collapsed in court.

### Interpreters

Among the innovations in Italy's new Code of Criminal Procedure, which came into force on 24 October 1989, are the provisions which guarantee the right of people whose mother tongue is not Italian to the help of an interpreter, free of charge. This should enable an accused person to understand the charges and follow the proceedings. Both Dr Clemente of DIGOS and Dr D'Angelo of the Ostia police told me of these provisions, but were unable to tell me how to find an interpreter for an interview. None of the files I saw indicated that the dialogue had been translated, even though none of the immigrants I had interviewed myself had spoken good Italian, and Dr Clemente himself commented during our interview on the language difficulties faced by all the immigrants his department came in contact with. His staff, he said, did not receive any cultural awareness training. All these factors suggest that interpreters' services are not generally used.

In particular, Dr Clemente said he had witnessed many ridiculous situations where the immigrants did not realise that the police officers were referring to them. (This is because there are two ways of addressing a person in Italian – the familiar *tu* form, which immigrants habitually use, and the more formal *lei*, which is in the third person, and which requires different structures in a sentence and inflections from the *tu* form.) Police officers would use *lei*.

## The role of the prosecution service

The way the public prosecution service operates has important consequences for both sentencing and public awareness of the nature and frequency of racist crimes. Unfortunately, it lets most perpetrators go free, and prevents all the evidence in a racial incident from emerging in open court. The problem lies in *patteggiamento* or the process of negotiation between prosecution and defence. If the defendants admit their crimes and agreement is reached with the public prosecutor on the appropriate sentence, the proceedings are short-ened. The aggravating circumstance of a racist motive, and the reduction of the sentence by one-third (which is applied whenever the parties resort to *patteggiamento*) are taken into account. No trial then takes place and there is no cross-examination of the victim, the witnesses or the defendants them-selves. In effect, the public prosecutor decides the sentence.

There was much publicity for one such case, a racist attack on Ali Saadani on 9 February 1994. He was first beaten up on a bus and then chased by a gang of about 50 skinheads. Those who caught up with him kicked and stabbed him while the others watched and cheered. Ali was taken to hospital with three fractured ribs and bruises all over his body. Within 30 hours, 11 people, three of them minors and eight youths of around 20 years of age, were arrested and charged with complicity in attempted murder, with the aggravating circumstance of a racist motive. On the day of their arrest, some of their parents were reported in the national press to have threatened the police for imprisoning Italians who were, they said, only defending the nation from blacks. The public prosecutor in the case, Giovanni Salvi, decided to go for *patteggiamento*. He negotiated sus-pended sentences of one year and six months each, and immediate release from jail.

The excuse for this very lenient treatment was that the accused were young, had no previous criminal record and, while in prison awaiting trial, had repented and given the names of other 'naziskins'. Also, they had freely admitted that they had acted purely out of racial hatred:

> We beat him up because he was dark-skinned; we shouted at him, 'You bastard dirty negro, go away from Italy', and we beat him up.

The prosecutor took this to mean that they had understood the gravity of their behaviour. The accused were all released, having spent only nine days in prison, and their sentences were not to be entered on their penal records.

There was an outcry against the handling of this case. Mr Salvi had accepted that the incident was really serious, when he made his final speech:

Ali was beaten without a reason, without having done anything wrong. He was helped by the bus driver, who let him off by the staff door. But the boys, not satisfied with what they had already done to him, pushed the emergency button and got off to chase the Tunisian and then to stab him, with malice, when he was already on the ground. The boys have not attempted to give any other explanation of this attack than that of the racist motive.

However, he went on, 'They have understood the gravity of their behaviour'. Defending himself against the strong criticisms which followed, Mr Salvi said:

Those who want to resolve public order problems in the courts make a big mistake. Excess only creates negative heroes. I have not been soft with Ali's attackers.[16]

In fact, speaking in full hearing of police officers, judges and journalists, the defendants and their parents had made openly racist remarks and had shown no willingness to talk about the reasons for the episode itself; their general attitude was to deny or play down any wrongdoing.

If the public prosecutor had allowed all the evidence in this attack to be heard, the public would have understood how such situations arise. Instead, Mr Salvi's view of the matter coloured the reporting. Evidently he believed that rapid arrests in these cases fulfilled the public duty, and that severe sentences were not appropriate in the case of perpetrators who were not acting as members of extreme-right organisations:

I have not been lenient. These boys are true racists, and they are a socially alarming phenomenon. They are not 'naziskins', but at the stadium they could become so. They are the reservoir of empty heads among which the violent and organised right finds its recruits. But they are not a movement. If one makes them negative heroes one only aggravates the situation and pushes them into nazi movements ... If one believes that in Ostia there is a public order problem unleashed by the presence of immigrants, the appropriate office must solve it. If the public administration has underestimated the emergency, it now needs to do something about it ... It is not the task of summary justice to resolve social contradictions. We are doing our duty; for every racist attack in Rome and its environs we have immediately apprehended at least some of the perpetrators.[17]

On the same day, the *Corriere della Sera* commented sarcastically:

Luckily in Italy there is not only the law, which punishes violence, and the police, who arrest those who practise it, but the courts, which know how to neutralise both ... It seems that now the law is advisory only. One can stab a Tunisian without being imprisoned ... For some time the courts have passed sentences which, for fear of attributing to individuals the faults of society, refer those faults back to society. And so they achieve nothing except to perpetuate the threats which burden society as a whole.

Three months later, on 15 June, the same pattern was repeated, when three men, aged 21, 18 and 18 respectively, were given suspended sentences of

---

16. *La Repubblica*, 4 March 1994.

17. *Ibid.*

one year and eight months and fined one million lire each, with immediate release from prison after nine days, on charges of a racial attack against Mr S Mabona. They had been accused of violence, wounding and robbery, aggravated by racist motives. In the courtroom they behaved as their lawyers had advised them – head down, no smiles and professions of 'sincere repentance'. Just before the Clerk of the Court was about to call for the start of the trial, their lawyers presented a handwritten paper by the defendants, which read:

> After these days in jail we have thought about what happened. We ask permission to address the victim to say that we have nothing to do with those boys called 'naziskins' who have hatred for people different from themselves, either for the colour of their skin, for religion or other differences. We are convinced that all the violent acts which happen in Italy or abroad for racist motives must be condemned, because they show lack of respect for human rights. We are ashamed of being confused and associated with this type of violent acts, which are far removed from the education and teachings which we have received within our families. We are sorry for the serious offence to the dignity of the Congolese citizen.

The public prosecutor, as was now 'customary', accepted the *patteggiamento* with the words:

> We mean to reaffirm a criminal jurisdiction which believes in the good of people, the educative spell in prison, the hope that the defendants having understood the seriousness of their act will give up forever behaviour which does not belong to our culture and civil life.

The victim was present alone in the courtroom, his lawyer having vanished. Nobody translated for him what was happening – what about the interpreter who, by law, should have been present? – but in his slang Italian he was allowed by the judge to stand up and say:

> I do not agree with the sentence. I did not invent the insults. I did not do anything. I cannot play basketball anymore, my knees and back are in pieces. What does it mean, small injury? I am frightened to go out alone at night and I wake up suddenly in the night.[18]

This happened at a time when racist attacks were almost a daily occurrence in Rome. Anyone perceived to be different was at risk, and within 24 hours of the sentence being passed in the Mabona case, two long-haired Italian students were attacked.

It is still widely believed in Italy that parents are the best people to deal with delinquent minors – at least, according to Dr Thomas and Dottoressa Manuguerra. In addition, all the officials I interviewed blamed poverty and deprivation on the outskirts of the city for racist crimes – the perpetrators, they said, suffering from poverty and lack of education, had no other way to express their discontent.

---

18. *La Repubblica*, June 1994

# STATUTORY RESPONSES FROM OTHER DEPARTMENTS

### Housing

Explicit provisions exist against discrimination in housing. Article 1 of Law 943/1986 recognises that all legally resident alien workers have the same rights to housing as Italian citizens. However, landlords have discretion to determine 'fitness to rent'. I could find no evidence of charges brought against landlords under this law.

### Social services and probation

There are two types of probation in Italy: the *messa alla prova*, comparable to the English system; and *l'affidamento alla prova*, which may be granted following sentences of over one year at the request of the convicted person. Use of this procedure depends on the offenders admitting their responsibilities and showing willingness to change their conduct. Dottoressa Spagnoletti of the Juvenile Court in Rome knew of two examples of *l'affidamento alla prova* being applied to 'naziskins': the probationary period was usually between one and two years, and there were regular checks by police and social workers to see how the minor was progressing.

Social workers play an important part in deciding whether the youngster will benefit from *messa alla prova*. The judge considers their reports. But this type of probation is not much used. Social services are supposed to be involved from the beginning when a minor is charged, but social workers are so overworked that the system does not really work. On 7 September 1994 Giuliano Zagaglia, chief social services officer for Rome, was reported in *La Repubblica* as saying,

> I have only six social workers to deal with 1500 under-privileged minors with parents in prison.

The situation was hardly better in April 1995, when I interviewed two social workers at the Juvenile Court. I was told there were only 15 social workers in their department for the whole region of Lazio. Consequently they were able to follow only 100 cases a year out of the 7,000 where charges had been brought in the Juvenile Court. They were supposed to investigate every aspect of the minor's background, to see how he or she could be helped not to reoffend.

I was able to see one report. It was on a youth who had robbed an *extra-communitario* street seller, with racist motives. The social worker who had followed him through the system and observed his behaviour in prison concluded that he would not benefit from his probation because he was not critical of what he had done.

One of the social workers told me they were given no cultural awareness training:

> If we know anything about other cultures it is because of personal interest and individual knowledge.

## Education

The Ministry of Education stated in Circular 207 of 16 July 1986 that:

> ... all those who reside on Italian territory have a full right of access to every type and level of Italian school, even if they are not citizens; any hostility or hesitation towards them constitutes a manifest violation of the constitutional and civil principles of the Italian state.

The circular envisages specific measures for the education of Gypsy and nomadic students. In Italy, all programmes in the compulsory schools affirm the right to linguistic protection for those with different linguistic backgrounds. Certain schools enjoy the right to offer bilingual education. Other minorities have cultural and language courses as a result of initiatives by various associations and bodies.

Recent years have witnessed a 'policy of diversity' in Italian schools, mainly those in big cities. Schools are becoming a focal point for anti-racism, organised by students, headmasters, and most importantly by immigrants' organisations in collaboration with a variety of statutory and voluntary organisations. *Extracommunitari*, Gypsies and Jews are beginning to visit schools to talk about racism.

There are at least two issues here: one is multicultural teaching, aimed at giving information about different cultures and promoting understanding and respect for them; the other is the question of how far the school goes in directly teaching pupils about racial violence and how the school authorities deal with racially motivated incidents on their premises. There is no state guidance on racially motivated crime for schools.

The multicultural activities of schools are very varied and cover a wide range of topics: not only racism, immigration, anti-semitism and the nature of 'naziskins' but also attitudes to homosexuals and convicts. How these topics are addressed is left to the individual teacher. Signora De Martino, a teacher who belongs to Senzaconfine, wants to move away from the discourse imposed by racists themselves and to construct a more positive approach. Unfortunately, however, there have been violent incidents in schools, emphasising the need to tackle racially motivated violence head-on. In one case, a 12-year-old Dominican boy was beaten up by three pupils in front of the other pupils at a Roman junior school. They were shouting: 'We will make you white'.

Neither the police nor an ambulance was called. Only the school janitor helped the boy, who had a broken lip and multiple bruises. After giving him first aid the janitor returned the boy to his class; his t-shirt was covered with blood. When his mother called for him at the end of the day, she asked why no help had been summoned. The headmistress told her that the incident had been only 'a boyish prank' and that it would not have been possible to lay charges.

I was also given some examples of Jewish children being discriminated against because of their religion. One five-year-old Jewish boy was punished because he did not cross himself during prayers in the classroom. The boy had to transfer to another school, and though the Minister of Education denounced the incident, the teacher responsible was not removed. The leader of the Jewish community in Rome has said that such incidents are widespread, especially in primary schools:

> Some primary teachers, explaining to the children why their Jewish schoolmates have to leave the classroom during religious instruction lessons, have told them that those children are different and will go to hell.[19]

Signora De Martino complained that meetings and exhibitions aimed at schools had achieved nothing; in her view they were just smokescreens for prejudice and discrimination which were widespread in the schools at every level and grade.

> For most teachers I know they are only a matter of having a day out; they fail to understand the real issues at stake. There is no serious training for teachers, no serious analysis in the schools of the very difficult concepts of integration and multicultural society, let alone sensitivity or understanding.

## THE ROLE OF THE CATHOLIC CHURCH

Monsignor Di Liegro, director of Caritas Diocesana, has always been one of the major advocates of the rights of immigrants. He is constantly on television and in the local and national press, condemning racist attacks as well as institutional racism and immigrants' lack of civic rights. He has condemned the failure to regularise immigration status and has demanded a new immigration policy to match admissions with job markets. To dispel myths about immigration, Caritas, in collaboration with other organisations, produces an annual *dossiere statistico* (statistical dossier), over 300 pages long, with facts and figures on immigration and the situation in different regions.

Caritas has provided services for immigrants since 1981. It receives funds from the Catholic Church and some independent donations. It employs some people but works mainly through volunteers. It offers medical care, both basic and specialist, legal assistance, some boarding arrangements, canteens providing free meals, and an advice and guidance centre. It cooperates with other agencies working in the same field, but it concentrates on providing basic services and has no special programme to support victims of racial crime.

## IMMIGRANTS' ORGANISATIONS AND OTHER VOLUNTARY ASSOCIATIONS

A report by CENSIS in 1990 listed 266 immigrants' organisations in Italy, embracing 45 different nationalities, and 196 associations of combined Italian and immigrant membership.

---

19. *La Repubblica*, 31 May 1995.

The central issue for most of the combined groups is the protection of workers' rights. Usually these bodies have little formal structure and are associated with trade unions or religious bodies. They perform an important role in bridging the gap between Italian institutions, with their bureaucracy and complexity, and the individual needs of immigrants. Italian administration relies on many discretionary powers. Rights then become 'localised', varying from place to place. Voluntary cooperative systems have helped to fill the gap, substituting in some ways for the social services that the public sector is failing to provide. Mayor Rutelli has complained of the government's failure here:

> Not a penny has been allocated to solve the many problems of immigration. It is talked about only as a problem of public order... the government lets the problem rot so that it can be used demagogically at election times. The problems in the end fall on the shoulders of the town councils, which have insignificant resources at their disposal and which manage the problems according to their political orientation.[20]

Voluntary organisations are then left to pick up the pieces.

The immigrant organisations, on the other hand, most of which were formed after 1986, concentrate on activities intended to safeguard their culture. Usually they are not single-nationality groups but mixed associations of, for example, Moroccans and Senegalese. They seldom include refugees, domestic workers, temporary workers or the unemployed, and their members tend to be young, educated and well-qualified. Their forms of organisation have been influenced by the trade unions and by left-wing Italian friends. These organisations have few relations with political parties and usually take no part in political demonstrations. The Latin American associations concentrate on culture and recreation. Groups from the Maghreb are concerned with religion, welfare work, and helping members with employment matters. Middle East organisations are chiefly concerned with what is happening in their countries of origin. Eastern European groups try to help refugees. And all the groups try to encourage mutual understanding by informing the Italian public about their countries of origin and their own problems in Italy, and by helping their own members with information about Italy.

## CONCLUSIONS AND RECOMMENDATIONS

The causes of racial violence have to be identified before one can deal it. Everyone I interviewed agreed that socio-economic factors were the main cause of racism and xenophobia in Italy. It appeared that the outer areas of Rome, predominantly working class and suffering from serious problems of unemployment, bad housing, an unpleasant environment without shopping and leisure facilities, and inadequate service provision and welfare services, are the most difficult and dangerous areas for black and ethnic minority

---

20. *Il Manifesto*, March 1995.

people. The problem lies not so much in competition for available social goods in these areas as in 'fear of the other' in such demoralised surroundings. And this fear is played upon by sections of the press and by some political parties.

Penal policy alone will not solve the problem of racial violence, even though trial and punishment can be important weapons in combating the phenomenon, by providing a useful deterrent – at least if sentences are not derisory – and by sending forth the message that society will not condone such conduct.

The political background has been of enormous importance. The right-wing victory in 1994 has contributed to increased uncertainty in society generally, but most importantly to the politics of immigration. A march organised with the explicit purpose of causing damage to a Gypsy camp was led by MSI MPs, and racist attacks have increased. In this environment, the police will not take strong action against marchers.

In Rome the situation is explosive. Many of my interviewees said that for years they had felt not governed but pulled this way and that according to the political flavour of the moment. The Italian state has too often been torn apart from within by corrupt administrators and politicians. Unfortunately, fascism remains an important strand in the national identity, and the increase in activity by 'naziskins' has been linked by many analysts to the election of people like Fini and Bossi.

## Recommendations

1. A reformed immigration policy, and implementation of the positive aspects of the Martelli law. This will require the training and employment of officers at border points and local reception centres, to provide crucial guidance, advice and support at the first stage.

2. Recognition of the rights and duties of immigrants as citizens.

3. Establishment of a central department, at the level of the Ministry of the Interior and Ministry of Justice, to collect and analyse data on racially motivated crime. Trained staff from both ministries should follow cases through from original report to charges and the court's disposition, by obtaining information from the police and the public prosecutor's offices. They should also liaise with police stations and the prosecuting offices on a regular basis in order to assess trends in attacks, districts of highest risk, and so on. This central department would also be responsible for disseminating statistics to the relevant agencies, and would develop policies on the prevention and punishment of racially motivated crime and on the education of the public to its dangers. Staff of the department should receive regular training on religious, cultural and social awareness and on immigrants' countries of origin.

4. The *Questura* (police headquarters) should create a Community Relations Department (CRD), with trained personnel, including black and ethnic minority officers. It should:

- take the lead in relations with Rome's immigrant communities

- take down initial reports of racial attacks and follow the investigations through, up to the trial. The CRD could also be responsible for cultural awareness training in police stations, especially those with the highest numbers of racial incidents.

5. Each police station should have a liaison officer responsible for arranging regular meetings with immigrants, local residents' associations and immigrants' organisations to build mutual confidence and trust. This exercise might eventually encourage more immigrants to come forward and report violent crimes.

6. The introduction of specific report forms for racially motivated crimes, to make recording and monitoring easier.

7. Interpreters should be available at all times during the investigation and trial. They could also assist at meetings organised by the CRD.

8. Forms and information on procedures and guidelines should be translated into the relevant languages, and posters in these languages should be displayed in a 'community room' at each police station.

9. Inter-agency collaboration should urgently be developed and given financial assistance. The police and social services both see the need for this, and could take a lead. Educational work is required to show the benefits of this approach as opposed to the present highly individualistic set-up where departments work in almost complete isolation.

10. The statutory services should seek the help of Caritas, which has succeeded in bringing some agencies together already. Caritas would be widely acceptable, as the Church's role is not usually questioned.

11. To meet the shortage of qualified and trained lawyers, resources should be allocated for the establishment of a pool of defence lawyers to work alongside immigrants' organisations.

12. Immigrants' organisations should be encouraged to find ways of tackling the problem of racial violence. One of them, possibly SCORE (Italy) which is part of the international SCORE network (Standing Conference on Racism in Europe) could establish a committee to examine this possibility.

All these efforts would need funding. Perhaps the best way to ensure the proper use of funds would be to invite the European Community to create a body to oversee expenditure. Racism in all its forms is a widespread problem in Europe, and to combat it effectively structures are needed which transcend national bodies. Work at national level is much more difficult because right-wing parties use the immigration issue during electoral campaigns to scare the indigenous population with imaginary invasions of foreigners. All European Community member states have, on paper, strongly condemned the upsurge of xenophobia, racist intolerance and violence on their territories. This condemnation should now be translated into the creation of effective bodies working in the member states to plan and control the situation. European Community action would not produce the same racist electoral propaganda which disfigures national elections.

## REFERENCES

*CERD Report 1995, (Italy),* United Nations, 1995.

*Committee of Inquiry into the Rise of Fascism and Racism in Europe,* European Parliament, December 1985.

*Committee of Inquiry on Racism and Xenophobia, European Parliament,* 1991.

Daily newspapers: *La Repubblica, Il Manifesto, Il Corriere della Sera* and *Il Mattino* were consulted for the years 1993-1994.

*Dossiere Statistico 1994,* CARITAS.

Examples of sentences and general files on racially motivated crime are taken from the Juvenile Court and the Rome Criminal Court.

*Legal Instruments to Combat Racism and Xenophobia,* Commission of the European Communities, December 1992.

Macioti, M I and E Pugliese, *Immigrants in Italy,*1991.

Marchi, V, *Blood and Honour, International Report on the Skinhead Movement,* 1994.

*Migrare ed Accoglie* (To Migrate and to Welcome), CENSIS, June 1990.

*National Conference on Immigration,* 1990 (all the reports).

*White and Black: Local assistance for extracommunitari,* USL I, 1992.

Research and general publications were also consulted at the Rome Archive of Immigration.

# CHAPTER FIVE

# A EUROPEAN PERSPECTIVE

Ann Dummett

## CONCLUSIONS FROM THE STUDIES

Despite great differences between the local situations described in Chapters Two, Three and Four, there are certain common features in the authors' conclusions and recommendations:

1. All emphasise the importance of the general political background. The German recognition that racism and xenophobia are a serious challenge to state and society alike, the work of the local administration in Frankfurt, and the attention paid to the 'Foreigners' Parliament', are commended by Anjana Das. By contrast, Colette Smith and Jolanda Chirico point to the encouragement given to racially motivated crime by the words and actions of parties of the extreme right, and the failure of other political parties to take the threat to society seriously enough.

2. All agree on the need for a strong statutory framework for combating racially motivated crime, but the Rome and Lyons reports suggest that implementation of statute law in those cities is far from effective, and that implementation is a key issue.

3. The central role of the police is evident everywhere. Victims' reluctance to complain, police handling of complaints, the police role (varying from place to place) in obtaining prosecutions, the police role within the justice system, instances of misconduct by police officers themselves, and, on the other hand, the positive effects that can be gained from benign police initiatives, all show the importance of policing in tackling the problem.

4. Other social factors besides racism have a powerful effect: the implementation of immigration and nationality laws; poverty, unemployment and social exclusion. These factors increase minorities' vulnerability, and may encourage hostility to them.

5. All agree under-reporting is a problem.

6. All would like improved support for victims.

## NATIONAL AND LOCAL RESPONSIBILITIES

It is more difficult to draw general conclusions about prosecuting authorities and the judiciary, because of the differences between national legal systems. In judicial systems generally, there appears to be a need for better information about minorities and the problems they face among all those involved, together with adequate interpretation in courts and police stations. The authors mention examples of lawyers being too few and too ill-paid to represent victims adequately: some improvement to legal aid is clearly widely needed.

Monitoring racially motivated crime is difficult everywhere, because of uncertainties about the definition of racially motivated crime and harassment, and in some cases because of subjective differences between police officers when they record crimes – and of course, as in Lyons, where the racial element appears not to be recorded at all.

To define racially motivated crime precisely, in a manner which will fit all national situations and criminal jurisdictions, is plainly a very difficult task, perhaps an impossible one. Even within countries, definition has posed problems. How do we distinguish the racial motive from others? How do we classify offences committed by children under the age of criminal responsibility, and so on. Perhaps it is best to begin from the other end: to look at the results we find so worrying, and then to consider if there are any general principles, which can be applied in different places, to deal with those results.

The problem is that some millions of people living within the European Union are vulnerable, through no fault of their own, to violent attacks, other forms of crime such as arson and damage to their property, and furthermore to threats, insults and acts of petty harassment, all of which are directed against them because of their perceived race, nationality or ethnic origin. The effect is not only that some of them suffer death, injury or humiliation but that all of them are placed in a situation of insecurity and anxiety, which in many cases affects mental health, children's progress at school, adults' performance at work, and each individual's chance of a modicum of happiness.

It is not at all easy for people who do not share this experience to imagine what it is like. But once the seriousness of the situation is grasped, it becomes obvious that measures must be taken, and urgently, to change it.

The problem for minorities has been compounded by the apparent indifference of the authorities, in many cases, to their plight, and at times by violence against them on the part of police officers themselves or by the failure of the courts to punish their attackers. At the same time, the public perception of the minorities has been largely formed by hostility to immigration. Immigrants and their descendants are people who are not really supposed to be in the country at all, it seems: they should have been kept out. From this viewpoint, violence against minorities appears a lesser crime than other kinds of violence, while harassment becomes just a means of letting them know they are not wanted and would do better to go away.

Rob Witte, in a paper prepared for the Council of Europe,[1] points out that racially violent incidents in recent years have attracted much national and international attention, and that in earlier decades such violence was seen as coming in 'waves' or temporary bursts, but that in fact it has been happening steadily for a very long time. The variations lie in the media reporting of it and the public perception, not in the phenomenon itself. Who knew then and who knows now, he asks, 'that 19 people of North African origin were killed in five arson attacks in Paris between September 1986 and January 1987?'[2]

From a British standpoint, one can ask similarly, how many people know that in Birmingham in 1948 a mob of at least 100 white men besieged and stoned a hostel where Indians were living; that one month later there was violence against black seamen in Liverpool; that the following year a hostel where black residents lived was besieged in south-east London?[3] It is widely believed that racial violence has increased in Europe generally since the late 1980s, and this belief may be well-founded, but we cannot be certain whether the last few years have seen a general rise in racially motivated crime or whether we have simply seen a sudden rise in concern at high level about it, stimulated by fears of an increase in popular support, in some countries, for extreme right parties. If the minorities in our respective countries have been suffering for a long time from racially motivated crime and have felt that their problems are being ignored by the public authorities, the first problem which good practice must tackle is to overcome the victims' disillusion and mistrust.

This task has to be accomplished by a combination of resources. At local level, efforts by police are needed to deal promptly and effectively with racially motivated crime to demonstrate good faith and efficiency. But such prompt dealing depends on the willingness of victims to report crimes in the first place, so a network of measures has to be attempted at the same time to create the needed trust and cooperation. Police everywhere will be the prisoners of the past actions of their own force: any instance of earlier police indifference to reports, or, worse still, brutality and violence on the part of individual police officers toward minorities, will put serious obstacles in the way of progress. Unfortunately, there are many instances, documented by reliable sources, such that minority members generally have long believed that the police cannot be trusted to protect them.

Efforts by the police are not enough by themselves to create trust or to deal with racially motivated crime. Prosecuting authorities have to play an important part; so do the courts. But all these institutions must rely upon a framework of law as originally laid down by a national legislature. Is the law adequate to deal with racially motivated crime, even if efficiently applied?

---

1. *The Nature and Causes of Racist and Xenophobic Violence in Europe*, Working Paper MG-EO (94) 29, Strasbourg.

2. *Ibid*.

3. Benjamin Bowling, 'Policing Violent Racism: Policy and practice in an east London locality', unpublished thesis, Sociology Department, London School of Economics, December 1993.

This is a matter which politicians have to consider. They have, moreover, to consider the whole scene within which the police and other local agencies are working, and ask what can be done at national level to improve trust and confidence among minorities and to discourage majority hostility towards them.

Other factors, as well as police indifference or malpractice in cases of racially motivated crime, affect people's willingness to go to the police for help. Immigration law appears to be an enormously important factor here: fear of removal from the country outweighs all else in examples shown in the Rome and Lyons reports. The police themselves are not responsible for the immigration laws they have to implement: national governments need to consider the effect on minorities of the threat of removal and the effect on the national majority, including police officers themselves, of categorising the physical presence of significant numbers of people as a crime.

It has often been suggested that police training should include information about 'other cultures'.[4] Looking at the examples in these accounts, it is doubtful whether such information would have made much difference to events. Cooperation with responsible local members of the vulnerable communities, together with disciplinary action within the police force against racist behaviour, might be more profitable.

The approaches of national governments differ here: some take racially motivated crime more seriously than others. To some politicians, and some police officers, racially motivated crime appears more as a threat from terrorists among the racial minorities than as a threat to the minorities themselves and to social peace and stability generally. But where racially motivated crime is taken seriously in the latter sense, the difficult task of developing good practice can begin.

It is virtually impossible to measure good practice. One might at first suppose that a fall in reported incidents of racially motivated crime would show success, but in the present situation the opposite seems nearer the truth. The problem of under-reporting shows through all accounts. Indeed, the Leicestershire Constabulary in Britain, which has made great efforts to deal with racially motivated crime (of which more below) regards a rise in the number of reported crimes as a success rather than a failure, because it indicates that the victims are putting enough trust in statutory authorities to make complaints. One can appreciate this rationale when looking at the reports, above, on Rome and Lyons. Given that there are numerous racial incidents throughout many European countries, and that all studies indicate massive under-reporting, an increase in reports of incidents would be an advance.

On its own, this advance may not take us very far. The next step is to ask how many reports are followed by prosecutions and how many of those prosecutions are successful. Information of this kind is given in the Frankfurt study, for example, but one cannot use such figures for numerical comparisons between countries, because definitions of racial incidents vary widely

---

4. Among others, by the Kahn Commission. See p 143.

and because the means of recording a racial element in crimes varies even more. Moreover, prosecuting authorities often have a large amount of discretion in deciding when to act.

A lack of reliable statistical comparisons does not mean, however, that assessments are impossible or that judgements must be ill-founded. The information in these studies of Frankfurt, Lyons and Rome, together with other information available, demonstrates some important points about current practice and suggests some ways forward.

The successes which Anjana Das points to in Frankfurt have been achieved by cooperation between a number of different organisations, some statutory and some voluntary. Furthermore, there has been a serious attempt to involve members of the victimised groups themselves in the process, both in helping the police directly and through the 'Foreigners' Parliament'. But it is clear that this cooperative work relies on a framework of rules and administrative procedures which have both statutory and political backing from the city, the *Land* authorities, and ultimately, the federal government.

Jolanda Chirico's report on Rome shows a starkly different situation. She records many complaints from workers in statutory organisations of a lack of cooperation between agencies. The minorities themselves have no effective voice and are not involved in the process of dealing with racially motivated crime. The Mancino law is inadequately applied. Although there are conscientious police officers engaged in detecting racist crimes, their efforts are frustrated by sentencing policies which repeatedly let offenders go free. The result here is not only to leave convicted offenders to repeat their offence, unworried by fear of further prosecutions (particularly since nothing is entered on their criminal records in many cases) but to issue a message to the public at large, including members of minorities themselves, that racial violence may be committed with impunity. Not only is the statutory framework weak and the administration hampered by unwillingness to deal firmly with young offenders: the political background is actually conducive to racial violence. This is because the MSI, a neo-fascist party, has made significant political gains in the last few years and in Rome has encouraged and taken part in threats to minorities, particularly Gypsies. In the north, moreover, Umberto Bossi's Lega Nord (Northern League) party has made crudely racist statements against African immigrants. The political response from other parties has been inadequate.

Colette Smith's account of Lyons reveals a failure to deal successfully with racially motivated crime, but here the context is very different from the Roman one. The processes of Italian government at every level are carried on with difficulty, are under-funded and unpredictable. In France, government is highly organised and bureaucratic. Red tape has fallen apart in Italy; in France it is tightly tied. In matters of racially motivated crime, however, the laws intended to repress violence are not working well. Nor indeed are the laws against discrimination, racial defamation and incitement to racial hatred. They are very rarely applied. In Lyons, it appears, there is no cooperation between the police and voluntary associations; on the contrary the impression is one of opposed camps. The interviews with the police indicate indifference to the situation of young Maghrébins, the most vulnerable group. The voluntary associations themselves appear to be mainly concerned with jobs, housing, religious and cultural freedom and above all security of residence rather than with racially motivated crime. This is hardly surprising, when they have no powers to deal with the latter nor opportunities to influence the administration of the law. As in Italy, the political background is unfavourable to effective work against racially motivated crime. Colette Smith describes the electoral advance of the Front National and the efforts of French governments to pre-empt that party's appeal by bringing in measures hostile to immigrants and people of North African descent, denying many of these the right to French citizenship or to security of residence. In this context, the efficiency of French administration is being demonstrated in removing people from the country rather than in safeguarding those who remain.

The three researchers were asked to investigate efforts against racially motivated crime being made by public authorities in the fields of housing, social services and education as well as policing, probation services, prosecuting authorities and the courts. The assumption that all these areas of officialdom would be involved proved to be ill-founded. This was partly because the structures themselves differ. Public housing in France, for example, is not organised in the same way as in Britain. British local housing authorities take overall responsibility for public housing estates. A more important reason was that Britain has been developing policies on racial harassment and violence for a longer period than have the other countries in question, and systematic efforts by the Home Office, local authorities and voluntary groups, with the work of the Commission for Racial Equality and others reinforcing such efforts, have produced a large number of initiatives since the Home Office produced its first official study of racial attacks and a report by the London Race and Housing Forum demonstrated the seriousness of racial harassment on public housing estates. There had moreover been concern about racially motivated crime well before 1981, with a number of local and particular attempts made to deal with it. In Germany, the systematic approach exemplified in Frankfurt is more recent, whereas in Rome and Lyons there appears to be no systematic approach at all.

Despite some concern at national level, however, the British picture is a very patchy one, with great efforts being made in some localities, but by no means in all. Leicester City Council and Leicestershire County Council have set up a Racial Harassment Project which relies upon cooperation between these local authorities, the police, and voluntary organisations including ethnic minority associations. In order to encourage reporting of racially motivated crime, the police have agreed that reports may be made to any of these other bodies, which will pass on the report only with the permission of the complainant. They will, if requested, keep the complainant's identity confidential, reporting only that the described offence was committed in a certain area at a certain time. Emphasis is laid on efficient follow-up of these reports. The joint project is trying to improve information on racially motivated crime by putting together reports from different sources including the housing authority, removing duplication from these reports and basing analysis on them. To preserve trust and confidentiality, the police are not holding this information on their computer; it is in the charge of the voluntary associations.

The Leicestershire Constabulary assigns a 'grade one' response to all reports of racial incidents, so as to give immediate reassurance to the complainant and to deal with the matter promptly. When an enquiry has been concluded, the complainant is asked to fill in a questionnaire and to say whether the police action has been satisfactory or not. In 1994, 95 per cent of respondents considered the police service 'caring'. There is a detailed monitoring programme. One unusual and imaginative initiative is a scheme whereby probationary police constables spend a weekend attachment with an ethnic minority family as part of their training, so that the officer can learn about the family's life and discuss matters with them. (Each family is paid £50 to cover expenses and the officer gets a £10 allowance.) Race attack alarm buttons have been fitted in the homes of black people who have suffered violence or harassment; the alarm is connected 24 hours a day to a police central control room. Not only police but also Special Constables and Traffic Wardens carry laminated cards with a message in eight languages saying, 'We are trying to help you. Please point to the language you speak.'

Another local effort, in the London borough of Newham, is the work of the local authority, which has issued detailed rules and procedures for its Housing Department staff, warning that racial harassment 'should not be compared with inter-neighbour disputes, general nuisance or vandalism', which are experienced by people of all races – it means verbal or physical violence used against individuals of groups because of their race, colour or creed. The emphasis here is not on police procedures, though guidance is given on reporting incidents to the police where appropriate, but on support for the victims. Victims who come to the office or who telephone must not be kept waiting, must be treated sensitively and must be given time to offer explanations. The interviewer should not judge the complaint or make remarks that suggest the complaint is ill-founded. The Council will consider moving a tenant on a public housing estate if that tenant has been repeatedly harassing neighbours. In the case of a private tenant, the Council will encourage the police to prosecute, or in some cases apply for an injunction to a court. A leaflet is issued locally in 11 languages, including English, offering an investigation of the case, and specifying:

> We will only tell the police if you agree to it. If you wish to report an incident to the police, contact your local police station ... Nobody will be contacted about the incident unless you have agreed. But if you do want the Housing Department to take action we will need to speak to neighbours and witnesses.

(These few points indicate the character of the Newham initiative, but the whole scheme goes into much greater detail.)

Such efforts are not found everywhere, nor even in all areas where racial harassment is an obvious problem. They show, however, that good practice is not just a matter for the criminal law system; it requires many different approaches, working together. An important feature of the multi-agency approach favoured in Britain (and which can bring in social workers, teachers and others as well as housing officials and the police), is that it begins with an examination of the problems in a specific, local area rather than from legal definitions of incidents and the nature of existing structures. This is a general principle which can be applied anywhere. It can make use of existing structures, however much they may differ from one place to another; by putting the problem first, one can then decide whom to involve and in what ways.

Any such process will require time, money and political will. It will also, if the efforts made are on a small scale, and at local level, be effective only if there is some national backing. National action is needed, furthermore, if police procedures are to be scrutinised, sentencing policy considered and a lead given to public opinion. There are many practical problems in achieving cooperation between agencies, and a slogan of 'cooperation' or 'coordination' is not enough. National authorities can provide the impetus for making plans effective.

Colette Smith's report on Lyons shows how important it is to have the right lead at national level by describing what happens when such a lead is lacking. Her description suggests an appalling situation of entrenched discrimination against minorities in which the government's immigration and nationality policy, enforced by the police, plays a major part. To make the kind of efforts that are being made in, for example, Frankfurt, Leicester and Newham, would clearly be impossible in the situation she describes in Lyons. First there would need to be a change in government policy and a radical overhaul of police conduct. Even then, it would take a very long time for the hatred she describes among minority victims, a hatred not only of the police but of everyone from outside the wretchedness of the *banlieues,* to evaporate and be succeeded by trust.

To make this contrast is not to say that everything is perfect in the places where serious efforts are being made to overcome racially motivated crime. It is only to emphasise the point that concerted efforts at both national and local level are needed before one can even say that a beginning has been made.

The problem is not just to formulate policies but to ensure that they are universally applied. In Britain, for example, despite all the efforts touched on above, there are still racial murders which are not satisfactorily dealt with by the police and the justice system. The case of Stephen Lawrence is only one example, but it has received much publicity. In 1993 Stephen, an 18 year-old black youth, was waiting at a bus stop in south London when he was attacked by a gang of young white men. He died soon afterwards in hospital where his parents were not allowed to see him. There was an eye-witness to the killing. The area is one where an extreme right group, the British National Party (BNP), is active, and many people are frightened of giving evidence against BNP supporters. However, this eye-witness, although willing to speak, was not heard in court because the Crown prosecution dropped the case. Later, when Stephen's parents brought a private prosecution, the witness' evidence was ruled inadmissible by the judge. Stephen's parents and their lawyer have claimed that the police delayed investigation just after the killing, so that forensic evidence against suspects could not be obtained.

The police deny this. Whatever the full truth may be, black people in Britain perceive the whole story as one of indifference to them on the part of the police, the prosecution service and the judiciary. They also see the activities of violent extremists on the right continuing unchecked. All the efforts of thousands of people concerned to work against racially motivated crime are thrown back by such happenings. There are laws against incitement to racial hatred and against murder: black people want to know why they are not working more effectively. Such cases illustrate how great is the effort needed at every level to check racially motivated crime.

## ACTION AT EUROPEAN LEVEL

Is this a field where action at European level could help? Both Anjana Das and Jolanda Chirico believe it could. 'Many of the interviewees,' says Anjana Das, 'expressed the view that an increased European dialogue would help all policy actors to improve their policies and procedures.' Jolanda Chirico makes a different point: racism, she says, is widespread across Europe and to combat it effectively we need structures that transcend national bodies, because in electoral campaigns at national level the parties of the extreme right exploit the issue. Her implication is that the institutions of the European Community need not vie for votes with extreme right parties and therefore are able to form policies against racism more easily than political parties at national level can.

The point of European action is to achieve ends which cannot be reached by national and local action alone. The major European institutions which could have a role to play are the Council of Europe and the European Union.

The Council of Europe, with over 30 member states, is well placed to promote international cooperation, but has no legislative or coercive powers. It was founded in 1949 to promote closer European unity and to protect fundamental human rights. Its best known production is the European Convention on Human Rights and Fundamental Freedoms: this binds those states which have chosen to ratify it and has proved of great practical importance in protecting individuals from arbitrary action by states. The Convention does not deal directly with racially motivated crime, though it does provide in Article 14 that there must be no racial discrimination in the provision of the rights it protects, such as the right to fair trial, or to freedom from inhuman and degrading treatment). Up to now, efforts to extend the scope of Article 14 on racism have not succeeded. The Council of Europe's work generally seeks to promote, by informative and persuasive means, better practice throughout Europe in matters concerning minorities. A five-year community relations project, concluded in 1991, produced a report which dealt briefly with racial violence and harassment, among many other issues, and called for 'more adequate measures' for dealing with it, including better training for the police.[5] A separate report issued in 1994 was

---

5. *Community and Ethnic Relations in Europe,* Council of Europe MG-CR(91) 1 final E. Strasbourg.

concerned entirely with police training, and described training projects already under way in nine countries.[6] Answers to a questionnaire mentioned racist and xenophobic violence of these countries, and even among these three it was not clear that such violence was dealt with in the course of ordinary training for all police. This report recommended international cooperation in police training. But when one looks at the above studies of Frankfurt, Rome and Lyons, it is clear that a great deal of thought is needed on how to make such cooperation effective.

In 1992 the Council of Europe published a report by Robin Oakley,[7] specifically concerned with racial violence and harassment in Europe. It examined the situation in six countries, devoting several pages to each, and made recommendations to governments, the police, other public agencies, and community and anti-racist groups. Some of these recommendations are of a very general character while others are more specific. But the publication of a report by the Council of Europe does not guarantee any action by national authorities. The Council can recommend, it cannot require. It can help to create a climate of opinion, together with independent studies like those of Rob Witte and others,[8] but action then depends on political will within countries.

The organisation to which interviewees referred in the above studies, when they proposed European action, was undoubtedly the European Community, which has the power to pass legislation binding on its member states. But the Community is limited by its Treaty, which defines the scope for Community action. Criminal laws are outside this scope. The Community is concerned with economic and social cohesion, and although this scope can be stretched to include a wide field of activity, it does not encompass criminal law systems. Since, however, the protection of human rights is among the purposes of the Community, and since it is concerned with education and training, health and safety at work, and the fight against social exclusion, it has room to develop policies which could help to prevent racially motivated crime.

This possibility has been greatly strengthened by an amendment agreed in June 1997 inserting a new Article 6A in the Treaty which allows the Community to take measures, if these are unanimously agreed by the Council of Ministers, to combat discrimination based on, *inter alia*, race or ethnic origin, religion and belief. Although the new Treaty may not be ratified for some time, the way is open now to Community legislation once that ratification has taken place. The main importance of the amendment for the time being is that it constitutes an important gesture, and that it puts racism on the agenda of the Community for the future.

There are other possibilities in the structure of the European Union (EU). The EU and the Community comprise the same countries, but they are

6. *Police Training concerning Migrants and Ethnic Relations*, Council of Europe, Strasbourg, 1994.

7. Robin Oakley, *Report on Racial Violence and Harassment in Europe*, MG-CR (91) 3 rev. 2, Council of Europe, Strasbourg, 23 September 1992.

8. Tore Björgo and Rob Witte (eds), *Racist Violence in Europe*, Macmillan, London 1993.

legally distinct entities. The Community was founded in 1957, with its institutions including the European Commission, the Parliament, the Court of Justice, the Economic and Social Council and the Council of Ministers. The whole is designed to achieve a balance of powers and to provide a degree of openness and democratic control. The EU was established at Maastricht in 1991, as a structure with three 'pillars', of which the Community is the first. The second pillar is for a common foreign and defence policy, which is implemented through the Western European Union. The third is found in Article K of the Union Treaty and deals with immigration policy and police and judicial cooperation. Here it would seem is the obvious place for European cooperation on racially motivated crime.

The amendments agreed at Amsterdam in June included a new Article K1. This says:

> Without prejudice to the powers of the European Community, the Union's objective in developing common action among the Member States in the fields of police and judicial cooperation in criminal matters shall be to provide citizens with a high level of safety within an area of freedom, security and justice.
>
> That objective shall be achieved both by preventing and combating racism and xenophobia and by preventing and combating crime, trafficking in persons and offences against children, illicit drug trafficking and illicit arms trafficking, corruption and fraud, through:
>
> • closer cooperation between police forces, customs authorities and other competent authorities in the Member States, both directly and through Europol ...
>
> • closer cooperation between judicial and other competent authorities of the Member States ...
>
> • approximation, where necessary, of rules on criminal matters in the Member States ...

Cross-border activities of neo-nazis and other extreme racist groups, the dissemination on the internet and by other means of material encouraging racial violence, and measures of cooperation in judicial policy on racially motivated crime could all be tackled under Article K. There could also be cooperation on police training. It is encouraging that the combat against racism and xenophobia has been placed first among the list of objectives here.

These changes to the Treaty, under the first and third pillars, would probably not have happened without the concentrated lobbying, over the last seven years or so, of dedicated campaigners from voluntary organisations and also from within the membership of official bodies: members of the Economic and Social Committee, members of the European Parliament and some officials within the European Commission. In 1994, the European Commission produced a White paper which called for 'serious consideration' to be given, the next time the European Treaties were revised, 'to the introduction of a specific reference to combating discrimination on the grounds of race, religion, age and disability'. Also in 1994, the EC's heads of government, meeting in Corfu in June, established a Consultative Commission, chaired by Jean Kahn from France, to devise, as a matter of urgency, a European strategy against racism and xenophobia and report within a year. The Kahn Commission reported back before the heads of government meeting of June 1995, strongly urging a 'race' amendment to the Treaty and submitting a form of words for it.[9]

The Kahn Commission's subcommittee on Police and the Justice System recommended not only measures directly affecting criminal justice but action against racism and xenophobia on many fronts: equal opportunities in employment, job creation schemes, freedom of movement throughout the Union for foreigners legally resident in one member state, the harmonisation of national controls over racist material, and:

> ... a duty on all those involved in the Criminal Justice System not to discriminate in the discharge of their duties. Information and statistics should be collated and published to help those involved in such work to avoid discriminating. In crimes where racial motivation is believed to be a factor, that should be drawn to the attention of the relevant court by the prosecuting authorities so that sentences can reflect with suitable severity the view which society takes of those involved in racist crimes.

The Kahn report approved of further cooperation between states in police training under the third pillar procedures and considered that racist and xenophobic crimes should be part of Europol's mandate. It emphasised the need to take account of existing work by academic experts and of international human rights instruments. On judicial cooperation it was more hesitant, proposing a questionnaire to explore countries' policies and practices. The report as a whole demonstrated the difficulties of international cooperation under the third pillar, as much by what it omitted as by what it proposed. Its stronger proposals all came under the first pillar, Community action. In particular, Kahn saw a 'race' amendment to the Treaty as crucially important (though the British representative in the group entered a dissenting minority report here).

The summit meeting of June 1995 did nothing to take forward any of the Kahn recommendations, except for one which proposed a European Observatory or monitoring centre to coordinate information on national, racial and ethnic minorities, produce reliable statistics in a form comparable between countries, work towards agreed definitions, and promote research and the exchange of information. Such a monitoring centre could, when established, greatly assist international exchanges of information and training on racially motivated crime. The Community approved a Regulation on 2 June setting up the Centre, which will be based in Vienna and run by a Board drawn from all EC countries, with participation also by the Council of Europe.

The new Centre, the new Article K1, and the new competence to deal with racism which the Community will be able to use once the Treaty is ratified could work together to tackle the problem of racially motivated crime. Community funding could assist training schemes and exchanges which made good use of best practice in different localities. Community action could also give a psychological boost to existing efforts, and perhaps help with the confidence-building which this study has suggested is essential to

---

9. *Report of the Consultative Commission on Racism and Xenophobia*, SN 2129/95 European Union.

any progress. Moreover, people working in the Community institutions are already familiar with the problem of adapting measures to widely differing national attitudes and situations. The Commission and the Parliament have both been urging strongly for some years that action be taken on racism and xenophobia. They have the will to act. But ultimately the power to act rests with national politicians. It is they, in the Council of Ministers, who are empowered to amend the Treaty, to pass Community legislation and, wearing different hats under Article K of the Union Treaty, to decide on measures of police and judicial cooperation. These same Ministers in national governments also have responsibility for immigration and asylum policy, whether at national level or in a coordinated European policy. Within their own countries, they set the context for dealing with racially motivated crime. Their political will to tackle the problem is essential to a Europe-wide solution.

On a more limited front, local action can achieve much. Some coordination of effort might be achieved by the European Union's Committee of the Regions, bringing together representatives of local and regional government in all member states. This body has from its inception called for action on racism and xenophobia.

Action at European level can also be taken by voluntary associations. UNICE and ETUC, the employers' and workers' organisations, have already drawn up a set of standards on equal opportunities in the workplace.[10] In their turn, they draw on existing efforts in individual countries, in this instance on the Commission for Racial Equality's *Code of Practice in Employment*, *inter alia*. Other CRE initiatives, like its document on racial harassment at work[11] and its encouragement through an annual prize offered to the best local authority scheme for tackling racism, of new ideas for good practice on racial harassment, have already aroused interest in some other countries. With the support of the European Community these ideas, together with ideas from other countries could gain wider circulation and imitation.

Racially motivated crime and racial harassment pose some of the most serious problems that the EU now faces. It is less widely considered than mass unemployment but its dangers to the social fabric are at least as great. Much has been done to collect information on it and to discuss it at academic level; the need now is to use whatever information exists on good practice, and to act.

---

10. *Joint Declaration on the Prevention of Racial Discrimination and Xenophobia and Promotion of Equal Treatment at the Workplace*, adopted by the Social Dialogue Summit at Florence, October 1995, European Commission, Brussels.

11. Commission for Racial Equality, *Racial Harassment at Work: What employers can do about it*, London, 1995.

# REFERENCES

Bowling, Benjamin, 'Policing Violent Racism: Policy and practice in an east London locality', unpublished thesis, Sociology Department, London School of Economics.

Björgo, Tore and Rob Witte (eds), *Racist Violence in Europe*, Macmillan, London 1993.

Commission for Racial Equality, *Racial Harassment at Work: What employers can do about it*, London, 1995.

*Community and Ethnic Relations in Europe*, Council of Europe MG-CR(91) 1 final E. Strasbourg, 1991.

*Joint Declaration on the Prevention of Racial Discrimination and Xenophobia and Promotion of Equal Treatment at the Workplace*, adopted by the Social Dialogue Summit at Florence, European Commission, Brussels, October 1995.

Oakley, Robin, *Report on Violence and Harassment in Europe*, MG-CR (91) 3 rev 2, Council of Europe, Strasbourg, 23 September 1992.

*Police Training concerning Migrants and Ethnic Relations*, Council of Europe, Strasbourg, 1994.

*Report of the Consultative Commission on Racism and Xenophobia*, SN 2129/95 European Union, 1995.

*The Nature and Causes of Racist and Xenophobic Violence in Europe*, Working Paper MG-EO (94) 29, Strasbourg, 1994.